the sensuous intell

The Sensuous Intellect

edited by
Ross McLeod

RMIT University Press, Melbourne

Published by RMIT University Press, an imprint of
RMIT Publishing
PO Box 12058, A'Beckett Street,
Melbourne, Victoria 8006
Australia
Telephone 61 3 9925 8100 Fax 61 3 9925 8134
Email: info@rmitpublishing.com.au
http://www.rmitpublishing.com.au

Publications Editor: Brenda Marshall
Production Editor: Noè Harsel

Research and Curation

Ross McLeod, Patricia Pringle, Christopher Kaltenbach

Production Team

Ross McLeod, Alexandra Doughty, Belinda Paulino, Amber Stewart, Nilika Nammuni, Rosie Morley

National Library of Australia
Cataloguing-in-Publication entry

The sensuous intellect.

For tertiary students.
ISBN 9781921166440.
ISBN 1 921166 44 4.

1. Senses and sensation in interior decoration. I. McLeod,Ross.

747

Printed in China through
Publishing Solutions

contents

Sensoria

Ross McLeod

Over the past decade the practice of interior design has expanded to include a vast array of disciplines and practitioners who work collaboratively in ways which challenge our conception of the nature of design and the manipulation of the physical world. Recent exciting work in spatial design interweaves ideas, materials, media and phenomena in ways that engage our senses both imaginatively and viscerally. In July of 2004 the RMIT Interior Design Program at RMIT hosted the Sensoria Festival of Design Education which explored this contemporary fascination with the 'sensuous intellect'.

Sensoria was envisioned as a week long event which would encompass lectures, forums, exhibitions and parties throughout the inner city of Melbourne. For one intense week, the city and its network of venues, galleries, bars and design practices would play host to a series of events on the nature of spatial design practice. We dreamed of the city becoming the university campus, of design education erupting from the classroom and finding its rightful place within the fabric of the metropolis.

Upon registration attendees received a festival pack containing travelers' tips, tokens, tickets, invitations, directions, maps and essential supplies. Over the proceeding five days each individual was free to engage with the festival and explore the city of Melbourne, attending symposia, visiting galleries and design showrooms, going to cafes, bars and parties, meeting design practitioners, academics and students from around the world and enjoying the range of sensorial experiences on offer.

Sensoria lectures and events
Atrium space and BMW Edge
Federation Square

Photos: Raphael Kilpatrick

The Sensoria festival program was presented within three curated themes –
'phenomena, media and materia'.

Phenomena, curated by Patricia Pringle, considered the shifts in attention and
focus that are altering our subjective experiences of the contemporary world. The
location of much contemporary art and design practice lies in the gap between
sensation and thought. This has brought a renewed interest in the mechanisms of
perception, and new models both scientific and intuitive. Does such a shift bring
with it new ways of reflecting on the phenomenal world? What is it that we are
experiencing when we choose to see with a sensuous intellect?

Media, curated by Christopher Kaltenbach, examined aspects of communication
design and spatial interaction that inform the way we understand the built and
virtual environment. From the consideration of the manipulation of environments
through traditional spatial practice to the conceptual and theoretical potentials of
multi-media, electronic sensing and emergent systems, this forum explored the
nexus between information and experience, behaviour and space.

Materia, curated by Ross McLeod, sought synergies between our sensory
experiences and the manipulation of the elements that give formal, textural
and structural qualities to our cities, buildings and interiors. The scope of this
subject included the skills and knowledge of studio/ workshop-based practices,
the potentials of advanced computer-aided manufacturing, the challenges of
sustainable production and the spectrum of possibilities within the synthetic
specification of material properties on a molecular scale.

Each of these themes was explored through a series of symposia which asked a
range of professionals and academics to present and discuss different approaches
to the act of design. In concert with the symposia a variety of exhibitions featured
the work of undergraduate and postgraduate students, and emerging artists and
designers. The work on display was presented and discussed through a series of
floor-talks conducted by the curators of the exhibitions.

Photos: Raphael Kilpatrick

Manifest
Australian Centre
for Contemporary Art

Venues included lectures at BMW Edge Federation Square and RMIT Storey Hall, exhibitions at First Site Gallery, BUS Gallery, Conical Gallery and the Croft Institute and a momentous 'sensorial event' at the Australian Centre for Contemporary Art (ACCA).

Sensoria embraced a vast cross-section of practitioners, lecturers and students from across the spectrum of design and art disciplines. Collaborations were from interior designers, architects, lighting designers, sound designers, performance designers, fashion designers, furniture designers, graphic and multimedia designers, installation artists, projection and video artists, painters, sculptors, philosophers, physical therapists, environmentalists and chefs.

It took two years to organise and coordinate the Sensoria Festival of Design Education, two years of developing themes, inviting local and international speakers, booking venues and galleries, curating exhibitions, producing websites, printing catalogues, convincing sponsors and balancing budgets. The two years of effort then condensed itself into an incredible week, a week of fantastic presentations, beautiful exhibitions, amazing discussions, grand parties, extraordinary moments, late nights and early starts; a sensorial overload.

Now it is two years later and the week-long event has become a publication, another thing again. The essays in this book offer a reflection of the Sensoria festival; unfortunately not everyone who participated in the week has made it too print. The gap between event and documentation is not so easily traversed. However the book has found its own life and its own interpretation of the sensuous intellect. Some of the speakers and exhibitions have had their context redefined, moving from their original classification within the themes of phenomena, media and material, and finding a linking narrative next to other practitioners' work. Some authors have taken the opportunity to expand on themes they may have only alluded too within the symposia while others have reworked the transcripts of their lectures into defining artists' statements. The result is a rich array of disciplines and practices, a cipher of contemporary thought and a sign post for the direction of interior design practice in the twenty-first century.

Hormonorium Philippe Rahm and Jean-Gilles Décosterd, 8th Architecture Biennale of Venice, 2002　　　　Photo: Niklaus Stauss

phenomena

Brain Gym

Robyn Hampton

The brain is a highly adaptable and flexible organ. It is no different to any other muscle in the body. It can be strengthened and developed, even though building new connections takes time to occur. There are limitations to its flexibility such as age and injury, but there is considerable information to support the premise that at any age we can influence and reshape memory processes, movement patterns, belief systems and therefore our understanding and experience of the world around us. It is definitely a case of the more you use it, the more efficient and flexible it becomes.

A fantastic and redeeming quality of the brain is its ability to be continually remodelled. Activities that challenge the brain expand the number of neural connections. If we continue to challenge ourselves with different and more varied experiences we strengthen neural connections by turning them into 'super highways' or myelinated pathways. By engaging in activities that are new and unfamiliar, we can alter the shape and direction of neural connections.

Movement is crucial for whole brain development. John Ratey[1] states in his book, *A User's Guide to the Brain* that:

> motion is involved in almost every aspect of human experience: thoughts move from one topic to another, emotions stir us deeply. Language is essentially a complex semantic dance of the mind and tongue, a sophisticated form of motion that allows us to manipulate the contents of the world without laying a hand on them. To improve our brains we have to move our bodies, take action and get going.

Paul Dennison[2], an educational therapist, recognised the link between stress and body posture and response. He developed Brain Gym[3] in 1969 to correct learning disabilities. Brain Gym uses specific physical movements to improve communication between both sides of the brain, known as the cortex. They also improve communication between the cortex and the middle and back parts of the brain to ensure maximum learning potential is available. Brain Gym works on repetition of movements to build and strengthen more neural pathways where we make more sense of the world around us. There are twenty-six movements specifically designed to promote more efficient and rapid communication of information to all parts of the brain.

To be a whole integrated functioning person we need to have all components of the brain co-ordinating, communicating and cooperating together. The brain and body are in constant motion, and the body's senses feed the brain information, which it uses to form an understanding of the world. The more we activate those senses, the more thinking and learning the brain can achieve. Freeing the body to move and stimulating the central nervous system integrates the body and brain. Our own unique functioning sensorial system filters the necessary from the unnecessary information it receives. It is that filtering system that ultimately shapes our interpretation and perception of our world. We are constantly deciphering and interpreting this information, adjusting it and configuring it into some sort of order as we develop through life.

Movement is initiated from the brainstem and cerebellum in the back part of the brain. There are reflexes such as heartbeat, respiration, swallowing and blinking which remain for life. There are also reflexes that have a limited time span. They are a group of pre-ordained movements called primitive reflexes. They provide the training ground for more advanced movement patterns. They are present at birth and should be fully integrated into the body around twelve months of age. The primitive reflexes follow a well-structured combination of movements that build on top of each other as each set is mastered. Each reflex has its own particular movement pattern that trains and prepares the body to move into the next movement pattern.

As the infant grows and matures so does the central nervous system. Higher, more sophisticated regions of the brain begin to play a role in the infant's development, slowly superseding the pure survival aspect of the primitive reflexes. As this occurs early survival patterns are integrated or controlled to allow the more mature patterns of response to occur.

The postural reflexes then come into play; they are regulated by the cerebellum that acts like a recording unit of movement patterns. It is only as postural reflexes replace primitive reflexes that the child begins to gain control of the body and body movements, learning to cope with the demands of gravity.

Sometimes a person, for a variety of reasons, does not complete some of these pre-ordained sets of movements. These retained reflexes continue to demand first priority on neural pathways long after they should. In this case, the person moves into compensation patterns, setting themselves up for more stressful and tiring learning.

When a person has not developed according to the desired format that nature intended, the person adjusts their body movements to seek equilibrium. Any living thing in nature seeks balance and will devise any method to gain it. In an elaborate system such as the human body, it will develop other ways to perform tasks.

It's these compensation patterns that can create an extra burden on the body. If a child retains some of the primitive reflexes, the sensory perceptions may cause them to process incoming information in either a hypersensitive or hyposensitive way, therefore, setting this person up for more stressful learning and behaviour patterns. During times of stress it is most likely we will operate from the reflexive part of the brain. When we are in this state it becomes difficult to draw on the wisdom and decision-making powers of the frontal lobes.

Stress can present itself in many forms affecting the connection between the brain and body. Under stress the automatic body response is to lock up the body, preventing the efficient flow of information from one area of the brain to another. Generally the body tightens, jamming up muscles, tendons and ligaments. Movement becomes less fluid, more rigid, emotions can run high with anxiety and self-doubt, and an overwhelming sense of inadequacy and fear can unfold.

A Brain Gym practitioner recognises these compensation patterns and uses a series of exercises to encourage the person to move in a more energy efficient and integrated way, helping unlock the body by releasing tense muscles, filling in developmental gaps and creating new learning pathways. Learning acquired under stress is easily forgotten and is not fully assimilated into the long-term memory.

If, for example, we have not integrated the Palmer reflex, a reflex designed to grasp and release objects, then particular compensation patterns will be noticed. Effects are poor manual dexterity of thumb and finger movements, poor pencil grip, hypersensitivity in the palm of the hand and quite possibly chewing type movements of the mouth, while trying to write or draw.

The physical characteristic when using a pen or pencil is that the grip continues to tighten with increased pressure of the pen on the paper, making fine and controlled motor movement difficult. The focus is on the mechanics of writing rather than the content. The most likely outcome will be writer's cramp, sore and stiff shoulders and eventually a tight and stiff neck.

To compensate for this unintegrated Palmer reflex, the body will manoeuvre itself into a position it finds most comfortable. This person may prop his head up with his hand or rest his head on the table, or adjust his paper sideways. To an observer it may look awkward and uncomfortable. This individual employs more energy and exertion to complete tasks required by finger and thumb manipulation, than a person whose Palmer reflex has been integrated into his system at the appropriate time of development.

When compensation body movements have been adopted, specific movements are used to create a positive physical change. By releasing tight and locked muscles, we encourage better communication to all parts of the brain, allowing improved rational thinking, abstract reasoning and language communication to take place. We then learn in a more relaxed and calm way.

In the example of a retained Palmer reflex, there are a number of movements that help switch on the brain, so the body can then move in a more relaxed and smooth way, thereby improving performance. To improve pen grip we use movements such as the Neck Rolls, the Owl, Elephant 8s, Energy Yawn and Thinking Caps to release tension in the neck and shoulder areas.

The Owl re-educates the neck and shoulder muscle proprioception related to auditory skills. When this proprioception is re-established, the abilities to listen, think and access memory are enhanced. By relaxing and lengthening the neck and shoulder muscles, the left and right turning ability of the head improves, restoring the range of motion and increasing the circulation of blood to the brain for enhanced focus, attention and memory skills. This enhances binocular vision and improves saccadic eye movement. The Owl is an efficient way to release tension around the neck, jaw and shoulders and alleviates the desire to squint or stare, tilt the head or lean on the elbows.

Elephant 8s activates the brain to integrate vision, listening and whole-body movement. As with the Owl, Elephant 8s releases tight and locked muscles of the neck and shoulders. It improves short and long-term memory and assists with depth perception and eye-teaming abilities.

We have the power to change our brains. The human brain's amazing plasticity enables it to continually rewire and learn not just through academic achievement, but also through experience, thought, action and emotion. As our brains train, the tasks become easier and more automatic.

The Palmer Reflex
Photo: Robyn Hampton

I would like to acknowledge Julie Gunstone, International Edu-K Faculty member, who generously shares her understanding and extensive knowledge of Brain Gym with myself and many others in the field.

1   John Ratey, *A User's Guide to the Brain*, United States of America: Abacus Books Australia, 2001.

2   Paul E Dennison & Gail Dennison, *Brain Gym's Teacher's Edition*, CA: Edu-Kinesthetic Inc. Ventura, 1989.

3   Brain Gym is a registered trademark of the International Educational Kinesiology Foundation.

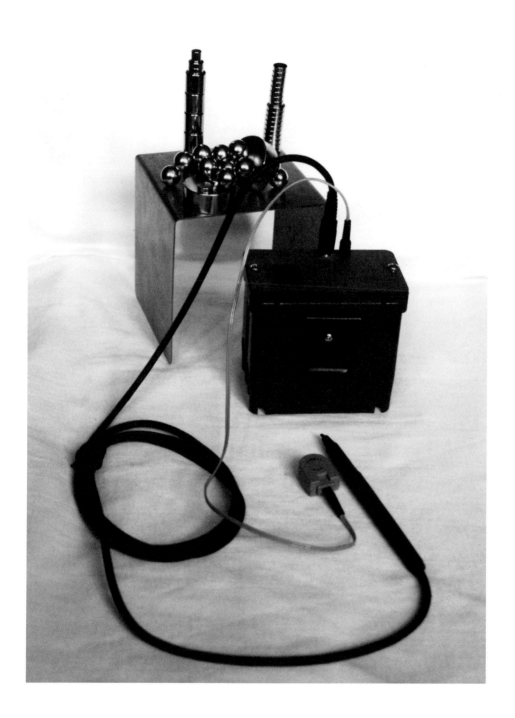

Perceptual Augmentation Devices

Ted Krueger

There is much of our environment that isn't available to us perceptually. Many will recall the description from their basic science courses of gasses that are tasteless, colourless and odourless. Among these are oxygen, carbon monoxide, helium, argon, carbon dioxide, neon, xenon, nitrogen, hydrogen and radon. In the case of hydrogen, oxygen and carbon dioxide, this is fortunate as it would be annoying to be aware of things so ubiquitous. Many believe that the senses are so distributed as to recreate a clear sense of the environment, but perhaps our ability not to perceive it is just as important. On the other hand, it would be occasionally useful, for example, to know if carbon monoxide is present.

In the case of vision, we often believe that the world is the way that we see it. Yet there are spectra that we can not see. In *Sensory Exotica*,[1] Hughes suggests that the proportion that we can experience is one over three times ten to the thirty-fifth power. This very large number, or extremely small proportion, appears to be the case at present. At some point in the past the proportion would have been understood to be close to one to one. The historical trajectory seems clear. To believe that the number quoted by Hughes is a final or absolute one takes more than the available arrogance. The accuracy of the number isn't really important, after all, what are a few orders of magnitude between consenting physicists? What seems clear from this is that we don't have access to any objective reality, what we perceive of the world outside ourselves is a limited view. That, which we deduce that it might be, changes with time and culture.

Animals can often sense things that humans cannot.[2] The compound eye of a fly might be made of a thousand lenses, but perhaps more interestingly, these lenses can simultaneously sense chemical concentrations. The trout has organs that allow it to orient within magnetic fields. The pits of the pit vipers are found on the head adjacent to the nostril and are sensitive to infrared radiation. Similar to the back of an eye but without the lens, this organ allows a heat image to be built up from the swaying movements of the head. These are naturally occurring 'night vision goggles'. That a bat navigates by echo-location is now common knowledge, but its sensory system was only discovered in 1938.[3] Bats emit an ultrasonic 'chirp' and then read the echo for the size and location of objects – especially insects. Each type of bat emits a unique sound, but all are complex, varying in pitch and intensity. This complex signal allows the bat to resolve objects of different sizes. Although the size of its ears seems an obvious hint, the dominant theory before its ultrasonic sonar was discovered was that it navigated by touch. This may seem to be a difficult (or ridiculous) hypothesis, but something similar can be found in humans.

Facial vision is the sensitivity to the proximity of objects possessed by some who are blind. It is described as a light tingling sensation of the face when the person is near to an obstruction such as a wall. Its operation remained a mystery for years. Some researchers went so far as to anesthetise the whole face, but the feeling persisted. Facial vision was found to be an acoustic phenomenon that was not perceived as sound but was manifested as a sensation on the skin. Current research on this topic has indicated that the distribution of sound adjacent to a surface is not uniform – that low frequencies are intensified close to a wall and that this may be a contributing factor in facial vision.

Perhaps facial vision can be considered an aberrant or enhanced form of hearing. On the other hand, maybe the traditional five senses attributed to humans need reconsideration. Rivlin and Gravelle, in *Deciphering the Senses*,[4] describe a vastly wider range. Among them are sight-visible light; hearing-vibrations in the air; touch-tactile contact; taste-chemical molecular; smell-olfactory molecular; balance-kinesthetic geotropic; vestibular-repetitious movement; temperature-molecular motion; nociception-pain; magnetic-ferromagnetic orientation; infrared-long electromagnetic waves; ultraviolet-short electromagnetic waves; ionic-airborn ionic charge; proximal-physical closeness; electrical-surface charge; barometric-atmospheric pressure; geogravimetric-sensing mass differences; eidetic imagery-neuroelectrical image retention and vomeronasal-pheromonic sensing.

These last two are especially interesting. Eidetic imagery occurs in a percentage of children. It is an ability that is much like a photographic memory that is spatially situated. It is by looking back at the location of an event or object that additional detail can be recalled or extracted from the scene that is no longer there. This ability is found in very few adults and typically disappears in children with the development of language, though why this is so remains unknown. The vemeronasal sense is the ability to detect pheromones and is attributed to an organ that is located in the nasal passage. In the few that have this sense, there is no conscious experience that accompanies it – that is pheromones do not (in a way) 'smell' – but the awareness occurs nevertheless.

While *Deciphering the Senses* is not a scholarly text, Rivlin and Gravelle are not alone in believing that humans have more than five senses. In the anthroposophical tradition, Rudolf Steiner counts twelve in three categories, those that are physical – the senses of touch, life, movement and balance; those that are psychological – smell, taste, sight and temperature; and those that are spiritual or social – hearing, speech, thought, and the sense of ego.[5] A recent article in *New Scientist* categorises senses into vision, hearing, smell, taste, touch, pain, mechanoreception, temperature and interoception. Depending on the sub-categories in each, the number of senses ranges from ten to thirty-three with twenty-one claimed to be 'generally accepted'.[6] Guy Murchie lists thirty-two specific senses grouped into categories related to radiation, chemicals, mental facilities, feelings and a spiritual sense.[7]

Clearly there is a range of opinions and we cannot settle the matter here; however, we can say that our experience is our experience and our environment is what our experience tells us it is. These statements sound stupid and tautological, but recall that most people would consider our experience to be a rather direct transfer of the world into the head. Perception is of reality, they would say. We have seen, however, that we have at best a very limited apprehension and that which we do have is coloured by the number and makeup of our sensors. Other organisms and other people may experience things quite differently.

But experience and environment are too easily thought of in terms of senses alone. In fact, this may be an enormous error. All sensory experience is internal to the organism. Properly, you do not experience the table when you touch it, but the firing of your cutaneous nerves in conjunction with a host of other information including those senses of the self such as proprioception. The environment needs to be distinguished from the self from within this internal sensory flux. This task is complex and may well be the result of long experience and the acquisition of the necessary skills. O'Regan and Noë[8] consider vision to be a skill-based activity rather than one passively dependent upon sensory input alone. They use the term 'mastery of sensorimotor contingencies' to describe a way of understanding that seeing is an activity that involves the whole body. This theory of visual perception can be generalised to perception in general. It is the invariants in the sensations related to the movements of the body in conjunction with the invariants in the sensory flow that allow the self to be distinguished from the environment. This is what gives the impression that phenomena are taking place externally even though the sensory 'information' is completely generated internally.

The conjunction of the sensory and motor is not only a logical necessity but is a neurological feature. Vittorio Gallese and colleagues have identified specific areas of the brain that integrate motor, visual, auditory and somatosensory inputs for the purpose of taking action within the space that surrounds the organism (in their case a monkey). This processing occurs at a rather basic level and is immediate. Rather than a second order cognitive function, multimodal sensorimotor integration for both perception and action is a fundamental feature of the brain. The specific organisations that have been found suggest that perception and action are related such that action is necessary for perception and that perception is fundamentally to serve action. It also shows that the sensorimotor contingency theory may have some basis in the organisation and operation of the brain.[9]

Portions of those neurological structures that are devoted to perception and action are active when the organism observes actions in others in ways that seem identical to when the organisation performs those actions itself. Gallese and Lakhoff suggest that this activation, or 'simulation' in their terms, forms the basis for much of our social interaction including empathy and learning by emulation. In addition, our conceptual frameworks are grounded in exactly these sensorimotor interactions.[10] What were formerly assumed to be abstractions and idealisations are now understood to be concepts directly based on embodiment.[11]

To turn to a theme of the Sensoria conference, the 'sensuous intellect' is grounded in sensorimotor interactions; as Varela observes, 'cognition depends upon the kinds of experience that come from having a body with various sensori-motor capacities and that these individual sensori-motor capacities are themselves embedded in a more encompassing biological, psychological and cultural context'.[12] By understanding the nature of perception, it may be possible to intervene technologically in a manner that will enable us to experience a richer world. Lenay and colleagues have studied sensory substitution, a technique pioneered by Paul Bach-y-Rita that allows for deficiencies from the normal complement of senses to be ameliorated through the use of interface technologies. In *Technology and Perception*,[13] they 'wish to show in particular that cognitive technologies...give rise to new modes of perception... – that technologies actually constitute human experience by generating new domains of what is possible with unexpected consequences'.

Bach-y-Rita's work[14] since the 1970s has shown that a sensorimotor skill-based approach to perception is empirically sound. The work was not intended to be such a demonstration; rather, what was sought was a way to assist the blind by developing a cutaneous interface to video imagery. Initially this was undertaken by building an array of tactors that vibrated on the back. It was found that under certain conditions patients were able to perceive the things recorded by the camera and to localise them properly in space. Eventually, the thigh, abdomen, forehead, fingertip and tongue were used successfully.[15] Bach-y-Rita and colleagues found that central to the ability to externalise the stimulus was the ability of the patient to move under free will and then externalisation only occurred after many hours of experience with the apparatus.

While this work is frequently described as seeing through the skin, I believe that the work demonstrated instead that it is possible to augment perception with technology and to create the equivalent of new sense modalities. If we consider the situation from the standpoint of the blind subject in Bach-y-Rita's experiments, a completely new way of perceiving has been developed. This is not 'seeing' as we know it and it is more important to understand that a wide range of possibilities has been opened than to believe that one has made the blind see (even though this has great cultural capital).

Devices

These ideas are guiding a research project to design and build prototype devices that have as their objective the extension of our perceptual abilities. In order to situate this work it is necessary to understand the relationship between an organism and its environment relative to perception.

A cutaneous interface has been chosen for the initial prototypes to make use of the existing body of knowledge in sensory substitution systems, and in addition, to allow normal sense modalities to remain operational while targeting under or intermittently used sensory capacity on the surface of the skin. The cutaneous interface allows new sensing capability to augment rather than replace existing senses. Keeping existing perceptual channels free to corroborate the new sensations is an objective of the device design. It is recognised a priori that the objective of this research is not in the production of the 'prosthetic senses' as technological artifacts or as isolated sensations, but rather, in the ways in which the new percepts augment and modify the apprehension of the world given by existing sensory modalities.

Several initial devices have been developed and are undergoing testing in the lab. The first device was produced as a simple demonstration for a seminar conducted by the author. It consisted of a photosensor mounted on a pair of reading glasses' with output via a small vibrator mounted to one of the lenses. The results were poor because the glasses' interface was intolerable for the ten to fifteen hours of use that are typically required for the externalisation of the percept. This experiment was important in that it developed awareness that the specific experience of the interface may well supersede all theoretical notions. It indicated that development of this kind of interface will be first and foremost a design problem.

The second device was based on a digital magnetic sensing technology used in automotive compasses. The purpose of the belt was to interface with immersive magnetic fields, those that are large with respect to the body. The output of the sensor was mapped to eight vibrators contained in an elastic belt. Global magnetic north was indicated by the vibration in the belt. Initial field testing took place in Melbourne, Australia. While the belt worked generally as expected, it was on an electric commuter train that the large scale dynamic magnetic fields surrounding the electric motors and lines could be felt.

A third device was developed specifically for smaller magnetic fields that are object-like with respect to the user. The movements that are required are haptic rather than locomotive. In this case, magnetic sensor input was transduced to a vibratory tactor located on the sternum.

The most recent design consists of a glove that contains a fingertip sensor that picks up fluctuating electric fields by induction. These signals are amplified and applied to the back of the finger by a vibro-tactile transducer that is identical to the one above. While, the vibrations are applied to the skin that on the back of the fingers is relatively insensitive to location, the vibrations are also conducted by the bone that lies immediately below. This makes the vibration difficult to localise precisely. In something akin to a tactile ventriloquist effect, a tingling is felt about the fingertip, sensation is thrown to the point of focal awareness. Like a bone conducting headphone, where the sound is conveyed by bone conduction without interfering with normal hearing, this vibration does not mask the tactile sensations from the fingertip (unfortunately, in the prototype shown the glove does that).

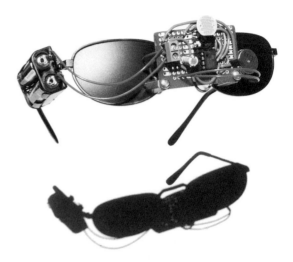

Photosensor Reading Glasses

Fluctuating Electric Field Glove

Photos: Ted Krueger

Immersive Magnetic Field Belt

The glove is intended to provide tactile feedback on the orientation, strength and frequency of the fields which the left index fingertip explores. The laws of sensorimotor contingencies can be developed through repeated use. The experience of these fields will be integrated into the full range of other senses in the context or normal activities. While preliminary results are quite promising the glove is presently undergoing testing and evaluation.

The design and implementation of 'prosthetic sensing' devices presently under development, is relatively straightforward, and has been given clear direction by prior work in sensory substitution. Instead of hardware development, the research focus is to understand the relation between the sensors, the kinds of information that it can deliver and the manner in which that information is applied to the body in order to give rise to a perception that captures salient dimensions of the phenomena. This is fundamentally an iterative design problem. In addition to specific devices, we expect to produce an accumulated body of experience that can be used to generate the principles by which arbitrarily chosen sensor technologies can be interfaced to the human body with particular attention to the qualitative aspects of the experience.

1 H Hughes, *Sensory Exotica, the World Beyond Human Senses*, Cambridge, MA: MIT Press, 1999.

2 *Sensory Exotica* is a compendium of information about animal senses.

3 D Griffin, *Listening in the Dark: The Acoustic Orientation of Bats and Men*, New Haven: Yale University Press, 1958.

4 R Rivlin and K Gravelle, *Deciphering the Senses: The Expanding World of Human Awareness*, New York: Simon & Schuster, 1984.

5 A Soesman, *The Twelve Senses*, Gloucestershire: Hawthorne Press, 1990.

6 B Durie, 'Doors of perception', *New Scientist*, 29 January 2005.

7 G. Murchie, *The Seven Mysteries of Life: An Exploration in Science and Philosophy*, Boston: Houghton Mifflin, 1978.

8 J O'Regan and A Noë, 'A sensorimotor account of vision and visual consciousness', *Behavioral and Brain Sciences* 24 (5), 2001, 883-917.

9 V Gallese and G Lakoff, 'The brain's concepts: the role of the sensory-motor system in conceptual knowledge', *Cognitive Neuropsychology*, 21, 2005 available at http://www.unipr.it/~gallese/PCGNSIOBA9.pdf (accessed 29 Jun 06)

see also

V Gallese, 'Embodied simulation: from neurons to phenomenal experience', *Phenomenology and the Cognitive Sciences* 4, 2005, 23-48.

10 V Gallese and G Lakoff, 2005.

11 G Lakoff and R Nuñez, *Where Mathematics Comes From*, New York: Basic Books, 2000.

12 R Varela, E Thompson and E Rotch, *The Embodied Mind*, Cambridge, MA: MIT Books, 1991.

13 C Lenay, S Canu and P Villon, 'Technology and perception: The contribution of sensory substitution systems', Second International Conference on Cognitive Technology (CT 1997). Aizu, Japan, 1997.

14 P Bach-y-Rita, *Brain Mechanisms in Sensory Substitution*, New York: Academic Press, 1972.

15 P Bach-y-Rita, M Tyler and K Kaczmarek, 'Seeing with the Brain', *International Journal of Human Computer Interaction* 15, 2003, 285-295.

Bridging the Divide – Transcending Distance Through Intuitive Technologies

Leah Heiss

All distances in space and time are shrinking. Man now reaches overnight, by plane, places which formerly took weeks and months of travel...Man puts the greatest distances behind him in the shortest time. He puts the greatest distances behind him and thus puts everything before himself at the shortest range. Yet the frantic abolition of all distances brings no nearness; for nearness does not consist in shortness of distance...What is incalculably far from us in point of distance can be near to us. Short distance is not in itself nearness. Nor is great distance remoteness. What is nearness if it fails to come about despite the reduction of the longest distances to the shortest intervals? What is nearness if it is even repelled by the restless abolition of distances? What is nearness if, all along with its failure to appear, remoteness also remains absent?[1]

The notion of human interpersonal experience transcending distance is a powerful idea generator for artworks, literary explorations and scientific endeavour. The abnegation of physical limitations has inspired adventurers and voyagers of all kinds since time immemorial. Until the last century connecting with people in remote environments was a time consuming and laborious process. Messages to be carried beyond the range of human voice were either conveyed by foot or horse and necessitated long lead times between transmission and reception of information. The communicational reach of humans has exponentially grown with the introduction of each new technology to the stage where we can now send and receive messages in real-time from an expansive range of places. Campanella[2] suggests that the advent of the steam train was one of the most powerful technologies to alter the spatial limits of the individual and allow for a renegotiation of the 'space-time envelope'. The subsequent invention of air travel collapsed the time required to circumnavigate the globe from Verne's fictitiously celebrated eighty days to a fraction of this time.

Today, contemporary technologies allow us to seamlessly connect with remote others from a far broader range of locations than ever before. While allowing us to transcend temporal dislocation, the barrier of different time zones, they neglect the spatial. This chapter investigates presence technologies which seek to address the spatial in remote connection through reintroducing a tactile element that is present in spatially co-present interaction.

Empathy Vest Leah Heiss

The *faraway* project, conducted by Polazzi, Jacobs and Andersen, investigates modes for connecting people who are separated by distance. The projects are founded on the understanding that presence is about being in the 'here and now'. That is, complete absence occurs when the significant other is occupying a different spatial and temporal dimension to us. Polazzi et al[3] suggest that intermediate situations, afforded by real-time technologies, allow us to reconnect temporally but not spatially. In this sense, the challenge is to develop presence technologies that provide a spatial and temporal sense of the remote other. The projects investigate the notion of an immaterial shared emotional space, which exists between people in intimate relationships. Technologies which allow us to enter this shared emotional space, despite physical separation, facilitate connection both spatially and temporally.

A critical factor within these and similar projects is that the proposed technologies are not attempting to replace traditional modes of communication but question whether a sense of intimacy might be enhanced through a peripheral presence indicator. The key to developing peripheral awareness devices is to connect people without relying on explicit language based media. Peripheral awareness devices facilitate the type of implicit understanding, between remotely located individuals, as occurs in face-to-face communication. Daniel Stern[4] suggests that the moment at which a resounding connection occurs between individuals is vastly different from the narrated version of events that becomes part of our conscious memory. He draws a distinction between 'awareness' and 'consciousness' by suggesting that awareness is an experience of implicit understanding whereas consciousness is awareness that has been processed for translation into language, a procedure through which important emotional information is lost. Awareness, in this reading, is comparable to the notion of peripherally conceived presence. It is at this implicit awareness level that the following projects seek to be registered, allowing users to reconnect spatially as well as temporally, thus transcending physical separation.

Empathy Vest – **remote environmental sensing**

The *Empathy Vest*, a prototype developed in 2004, focused on the use of simple technologies to facilitate an embodied experience of remote space and place. The project questioned whether through physically sensing remote stimulus (light, wind, sound etc), the user might experience psychological change. Philosophically, the *Empathy Vest* sought to create a sense of 'spatial empathy' between people who were physically separated. Spatial empathy was defined as 'the development of an implicit understanding and awareness of the spatial condition that another being is experiencing'.[5] The prototype encouraged 'spatial empathy' through the real-time transmission of environmental stimulus. Conceptually, the prototype questioned whether through establishing a real-time feedback loop between two people, allowing them to sense each other's environmental experiences, a deeper sense of empathy might occur.

The project was concerned with the creation of wearable information responsive environments that acted as transmitters and receivers of information. The wearable devices hosted a series of input sensors and output channels. The input channels, two touch sensors and one voice relay sensor, allowed the wearer to have a sense of experiencing informational stimulus mapped onto the body through the output modes: four light channels and one fan. The project was interested in the notion of emergent outcomes and thus the data channels were developed with a factor of chance in output combinations. The prototype was developed with a Programmable Logic Controller (PLC) microcontroller with multiple inputs and outputs, allowing for easy modification to incorporate new stimulus, depending on the situation being studied.

Samuel Natale[6] proposes a model of empathy that has three distinct phases: Interactive Empathy – which entails sensing the feelings of another and communicating these to him/her; Predictive Accurate Empathy – imagining oneself in the space of another, thus being able to intuit the fears, thoughts and emotions of that person; and finally Predictive Accurate Empathy with a Generalised Other – the ability to put oneself into the position of a large class or group of people. Drawing from this theoretical framework the *Empathy Vest* aimed to explore the final two scenarios – empathetically connecting with a single other and connecting with a group of people. It was devised with a series of user interaction scenarios in mind: the relationship between two remotely located individuals; between an individual and a remote crowd; and between an individual and a remote space.

Ether Beat – heartbeat as a communication language

The *Ether Beat* projects are a distillation of design concepts initially investigated through the Empathy Vest. The garments and artefacts focus on transferring the singular biosignal of heartbeat.

The heart is a highly charged icon in most cultures. In contemporary Western thought the head is regarded as the home of intellect and the heart as the domain of emotion, their diametric opposition reinforced by a plethora of sayings and clichés. However, this view of intellect being located in the head is not shared by all cultures. In the Koran the heart is used as a synonym for knowledge whilst the Wuitoto tribe from southern Colombia use the same word for chest, heart, memory, and thought.[7] McCraty et al[8] suggest that the heart generates the strongest electromagnetic field of any part of the body. Through the use of sensitive electrostatic detection devices this field can be measured up to a metre from the body. A series of experiments, led by McCraty, determined that cardiac electricity was registered in the brainwaves of proximate others, particularly when people were touching. The notion of extending this zone of active current beyond the immediate radius of the body underscores the *Ether Beat* investigations. Within this research heartbeat – usually a private internal signal – is externalised and used as an active communication modality.

Ether Beat encompasses a range of compatible garments that sense, process, transmit and receive the heartbeat wavelength (ECG). The collection is made up of two sets of garments. Each set comprises: a singlet (*Under Beat*) that houses the ECG electrodes and which connects to either of the outer garments: *Ether Scarf*, a scarf, or *Ether Beat*, a blouse. The under garments are enabled with ECG sensors while the outer garments house signal processing equipment, small vibration motors, and radio transceivers. The sensation provided by the garments is of wearing the heartbeat of your remote friend/lover/relative as vibration through your garment.

The garments utilise simple technologies, which have been 're-jigged' to suit the prototype, combined with specifically designed processing equipment. From a design perspective, the challenge has been to utilise the structure of the requisite technologies to inform the development of the apparel, rather than retrofitting an existing garment. In this foregrounding of the physical properties of technology, including the structural boning capabilities of wiring and the weight of the vibration motors, new opportunities for garment design arise. They have been drafted from the initial stages using traditional construction techniques in non-traditional ways to accommodate electronic pathways, processing equipment and battery power.

The prototypes aim to enrich the remote communications experience through reintroducing an embodied, tactile dimension that is present in face-to-face communication. They do not purport to replicate the complexity of the myriad channels at work in spatially co-present interaction but rather to introduce an element of peripheral awareness into the communications mix.

Under Beat

Ether Beat

Ether Scarf

Photos: Leah Heiss

Hand Hearts – handheld communication devices

The *Hand Hearts* were developed to receive the ECG signal being detected and transmitted through the *Ether Beat* garments. They use similar technologies to the garments but incorporate them into handheld devices. The devices are resin cast hearts, derived from an anatomical model, that are fitted with small motors which vibrate with the received impulse. The hearts allow multiple users to interact simultaneously with a transmitted heartbeat. Philosophically, they are designed to question how such devices might impact upon remote interpersonal understanding and encourage the emergence of new group ecologies. The hearts were also created to ascertain the variation in user reactions between receiving the heartbeat through a handheld (*Hand Heart*) or a wearable (*Ether Beat*) device.

Within user testing trials individuals responded to the experience of holding the beating heart in highly emotional ways. Following are several responses from anonymous users after interacting with the hearts:

'It feels like when I held my first cat. It was so little it sat in the palm of my hand. I could feel its heartbeat. This was when I was in grade six. The kitten was three weeks old – born under my grandparents house by a stray.'

'Whilst holding the beating heart, I felt less focused on my own heartbeat, but aware of my hands sweating and my level of mild anxiety, and having to sit with that.'

'Held in the palm, close to my wrist – bizarre, queezy feeling of recognition of self.'

While contemporary communications technologies have the capacity to mediate our relationships, they fall short of encouraging the richness of real-time collocated communication. The projects discussed here aim to address the limitations of remote communication by engaging a spatial dimension that is resident in spatially co-present interaction. They transmute internal processes into externally transmissible messages which are received by remote others through the agency of technology. As such they reposition the emphasis in remote communication technologies from technical issues (resolution, portability etc) to action at a distance, thus promoting new technologies which will allow us to connect physically despite bodily absence.

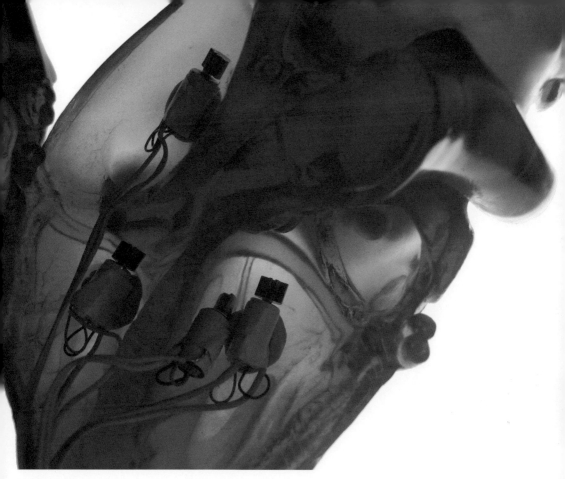

Hand Heart Leah Heiss

1   Martin Heidegger, *Poetry, Language, Thought*, New York: Harper & Row, 1971,163.
2   Thomas J Campanella, in Ken Goldberg (ed), T*he Robot in the Garden – Telerobotics and Telepistemology in the Age of the Internet*, Cambridge: MIT Press, 2000.
3   L Polazzi, M Jacobs and K Andersen, *Presence in the Emotional Space*, in Proceedings of Fifth Annual International Workshop on Presence Research (PRESENCE), Porto, Portugal, 2002.
4   Daniel Stern, *The Present Moment in Psychotherapy and Everyday Life*, New York: WW Norton & Co, 2004.
5   This definition was developed by the author and presented at the first public presentation of the work.
6   Samuel M Natale, An Experiment in Empathy, Slough: National Foundation for Educational Research in England and Wales,1972.
7   Jean Chevalier,Alain Gheerbrant and John Buchanan-Brown, *The Penguin Dictionary of Symbols*, New York: Penguin, 2000.
8   Rollin McCraty, Mike Atkinson, Dana Tomasino and William A Tiller, 'The electricity of touch: Detection and measurement of cardiac energy exchange between people', in: Karl H Pribram (ed) *Brain and Values: Is a Biological Science of Values Possible*, Mahwah, NJ: Lawrence Erlbaum Associates, Publishers, 1998.

Aural Culture

Lawrence Harvey

In the original presentation at the Sensoria Conference I related the creation of particular sounds and the production of spatial sound works to an encompassing field of technological, social and cultural conditions. It was an attempt at revealing the composite relations between ideas and their realisation as 'works' in the practice of one sound designer.

However theory has a tendency to make practice appear inevitable. In attempting to present a coherent narrative of ideas, motivations, projects and reflections the problem of flow arises. Should the presentation unfold like a proficiently edited film, or capture the detours, asides and spontaneous piecing together of thought? What a polished presentation lacks is a granularity that ensures an audience is exposed to the uncertainty inherent in doing things that may not have been done before, or new ways of achieving the known. How adequately can the *inter* and *intra*-dependence of the milieu and the work be described from inside by the practitioner?

Acknowledging this situation as one confronted by many, this text is written from the perspective of a sound designer and composer working in a school of spatial studies as opposed to the more likely scenario of a sound based practitioner working in a school of music, new media studies or acoustic engineering. This educational and research setting for sound based studies makes possible a broader focus on all aspects of human aural experience as the field of practice and investigation.

One task in teaching is to prepare emerging designers to consciously engage with the complex of real-world situations where they must know how to invent and maintain adaptable practices. Central to this are analytical abilities to observe and question what and how one is working, to find ways of investigating other ways of making and doing, essentially, to use research as a mode of learning.

For artists whose ideas are realised through sounding works, a plethora of production contexts are on offer, such as gallery based sound installations, concert compositions, radiophonic works, theatre and dance sound designs, urban soundscape design, games and other interactive media, CD, DVD, film and television audio production. With the advent of increasingly low cost technological platforms for spatial sound delivery in public, private and virtual spaces the opportunities have expanded to make work in formats other than the long-standing stereo one.

SIAL Sound Pod
Paul Morgan Architects
Photo: Andrius Lipsys

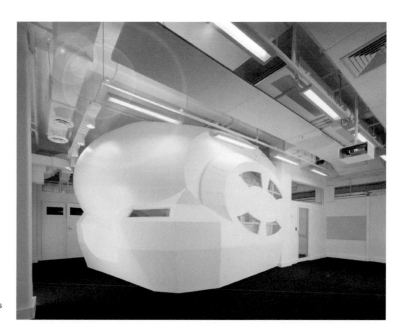

SIAL Sound Pod
Paul Morgan Architects
Photo: Andrius Lipsys

This pervasiveness of electroacoustic sound in daily life necessitates a framework for considering it against other dominant forms of cultural expression, particularly those grouped under the readily accepted expression of visual culture.

> ...The 'visual culture' approach acknowledges the reality of living in a world of cross-mediation – our experience of culturally meaningful visual content appears in multiple forms, and visual content and codes migrate from one form to another: print images and graphic design, TV and cable TV, film and video, computer interfaces and software design, Internet/ Web as a visual platform, digital media, advertising in all media..., fine art and photography, fashion, architecture, design, and urban design.[1]

In recent years, sound culture has emerged to describe the practice of artists whose ideas are realised through sounding works. But notice the difference. The term visual culture identifies an effort of the visually receptive sense and suggests an active engagement is required on the part of an observer, while the term sound culture doesn't establish the same relationship. Sound culture gives the impression that sound happens, but listening doesn't. Terms such as aural or auditory culture, as used by Michael Bull[2] carry an assumption of a listener present in the relationship.

Knowledge of the sounding world has historically been embodied within the disciplines of acoustics and music. With the emergence of acoustic ecology or soundscape studies during the 1960s and 1970s, the entirety of the sounding world and its relationship to listeners became the subject of a single field. Soundscape studies comes closest to integrating identifiable components of the sounding world through which we may actively '...navigate and negotiate meaning' as opposed to insensibly registering just the incidence of an aural stimulus.

Acoustic ecology is a widely inter-disciplinary field, built on knowledge from music, acoustics, psychoacoustics, sociology, bio-acoustics, anthropology, psychology and geography. In explaining how such a wide range of disciplines might successfully be integrated, its founder R Murray Schafer [3] and others invoke the idea of an acoustic bauhaus. The dream was that the practice of acoustic ecology would synthesise '...craftsmanship and artistic production, functionalism and creativity...' arising from an interdisciplinary teaching and design practice.[4] Acoustic ecology is the study of living beings' relationship to the soundscape. The word soundscape is:

> ...derived from landscape. Soundscape is the acoustic manifestation of place, where the sounds give the inhabitants a sense of place and the place's acoustic quality is shaped by the inhabitants' activities and behaviour. The meanings are created precisely because of this interaction between soundscape and people. Thus, the sonic environment (or soundscape), which is the sum total of all sounds within any defined area, is an intimate reflection of – among others – the social, political, technological, and natural conditions of the area. Change in these conditions means change in the sonic environment.[5]

This broad agenda differentiates acoustic ecology from other environmental sound movements such as noise and right-to-quiet movements.[6] While there is some debate about whether a phenomenological approach is appropriate within an ecological framework, I have found the listener centred approach of acoustic ecology, applied to teaching sound within an architectural program particularly useful, as it is predicated on a listener within an environment, and not a range of objective measurements of quantity. Through this approach, the student as listener is situated within the environment and his or her own aural experience is the basis of learning about sound. Qualitative definitions abound in acoustic ecology, describing physical conditions and their intersection with social and cultural conditions.

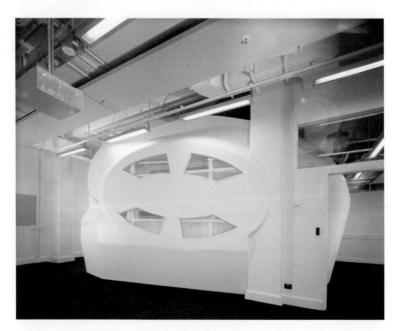

SIAL Sound Pod
Paul Morgan Architects
Photo: Andrius Lipsys

SIAL Sound Pod
Paul Morgan Architects
Photo: Andrius Lipsys

By way of example and returning to the rise of production contexts for spatial sound design, consider the notion from acoustic ecology of the acoustic horizon:

> The farthest distance in every direction from which sounds may be heard. Incoming sounds from distant sources define the outer limits over which acoustic communication may normally occur, and thus help to define the perceived geographical relationships between communities.[7]

And not just of communities, but also individuals. In contemporary urban environments, the extent of the acoustic environment has greatly diminished. In an oral history interview I conducted a few years ago on the Melbourne Noise Survey of the early 1980s, a local acoustician reported that in the 1950s, it was still possible to hear train sounds from Flinders St Station, while standing on Glenferrie Station. To a listener in 2005 in Melbourne, this is difficult to conceive, and unlikely to happen except under extraordinary acoustic conditions.[8]

Is there a connection between a collapse in the acoustic horizon, and the rise of spatial sound technologies and designs? I would propose a link exists and it is to reclaim a sense of aural expansiveness and detail, lost in our everyday experience in the built environment, through the virtual aural enhancement of the physical spaces we occupy daily.

Architecture and technology have been used to create enhanced physical or even metaphysical situations for listeners for centuries. R Murray Schafer in *The Tuning of the World* [9] discusses immersion in sound, in a section called 'The return to the submarine home' in relation to plainsong chanting in Norman and Gothic churches. Quoting Viennese sociologist Kurt Blaukopf, Schafer expands on the point that the long and diffuse reverberation times and subsequent impossibility of localising the sound makes the listener believe they are part of the world of sound. Quoting from Blaukopf, he notes, the listener does not '...face the sound in "enjoyment" — he is wrapped up by it.'

The most common form of aural immersion today is that of headphone listening. While in the architectural mode of immersion in the cathedral one is surrounded by a sphere of moving elements, in headphone listening, one '...is the sphere'. Without an acoustic horizon to orient the listener, the listener is the universe of sound. But without releasing the experience of sound, Schafer points out that the listener '...does not take his place again with humanity'. We are a culture that doesn't sing in groups in resonant spaces, and our daily existence relies on noisily traversing our environment and the dull drone of plant and equipment servicing buildings, cooling fans in computers and technology, and the hum of operating domestic appliances. It is as if we are silenced by the sounds around us.

Hearing is a continuous activity in human life, while listening is not. The difference is likely to be one of 'psychological demarcation'. A way of understanding the practice of an acoustic designer is to describe it as articulating the demarcation between hearing and listening. A mereological (part-whole relationships) condition is created – listening niches are made in the continuum of hearing.

In his paper 'The environment of mind', Barry Smith describes J Gibson's vision of reality as a whole, as '...a complex hierarchy of inter-nested levels of parts and subparts...' where:

> ...molecules are nested within cells, cells are nested within leaves, leaves are nested within trees, trees are nested within forests, forests are nested within Special Federal Forest Protection Zones, and so on. Each type of organism is then tuned in its perception and action to objects on a specific level within this complex hierarchy – to objects ('affordances') which are the environmental correlates of adapted traits on the side of the organism and which together form what Gibson calls the organism's 'ecological niche'. A niche is that into which an animal fits (as a hand fits into a well-fitting glove). The niche is that in relation to which the animal is habituated in its behavior. It embraces not only things of different sorts, but also shapes, textures, boundaries (surfaces, edges), all of which are organized in such a way as to enjoy affordance-character for the animal in question in the sense that they are relevant to its survival. The given features motivate the organism; they are such as to intrude upon its life, to stimulate the organism in a range of different ways. [10]

In my own practice since 1999, the types of listening scenarios or environments have included an urban soundscape system, a VR centre, various exhibition spaces, theatre performances, radiophonic broadcasts, sound diffusion concerts, a community noise survey in a games engines, and the establishment of a new sound studio.   Each of these projects can be described and compared in terms of physical properties (its topological milieu) and sound objects (affordances), human components (actions and experience of listeners) and the setting program emerging from the sequence of transactions between people and sound objects. Each of these settings are nested, bounded by describable conditions, and are niches within an overarching acoustic environment, they are designed to be composed of people and sound objects that configure in such a way as to carry out an experience or program within specified time-space boundaries.

1   Martin Irvine, Introducing Visual Culture: Ways of Looking at All Things Visual, 2005 http://www.georgetown.edu.au/faculty/irvinem/visualarts/Intro-VisualCulture.html (accessed 31 March 2004).

2   Michael Bull and Les Black, *The Auditory Culture Reader*, New York: Berg, 2003.

3   R Murray Schafer, *The Tuning of the World*, New York: Alfred Knopf, 1977.

4   Hildegard Westerkamp, 'Bauhaus and Soundscape Studies – Exploring Connections and Differences' (text of speech on line), October 1994, revised 2002. http://www.sfu.ca/~westerka/writings/bauhaus.html> (accessed 31 March 2003).

5   Ibid.

6   For links to other noise activism and right-to-quiet organisations, see http://www.acousticecology.org/urban.html, (accessed 31 March 2004), http://www.calm-network.com/ (accessed 31 March 2004), http://www.quiet.org/ (accessed 31 March 2004).

7   Barry Truax, ed, *Handbook for Acoustic Ecology* (book on line), Cambridge Street Publishing, 1999 (accessed 31 March 2004); http://www2.sfu.ca/sonic-studio/handbook/

8   Lawrence Harvey, Unpublished oral history interview with Graeme Harding, 2000.

9   R Murray Schafer, *The Tuning of the World*, New York: Alfred Knopf, 1977.

10 Barry Smith, 'The environment of mind'. Draft paper prepared for The Conscious Mind Conference, Buffalo, 5-6 November 1999, (accessed 7 February 2005), http://ontology.buffalo.edu/smith/articles/environmentofmind.htm

SIAL Sound Pod
Paul Morgan Architects
Photo: Andrius Lipsys

Hormonorium Philippe Rahm and Jean-Gilles Décosterd, 8th Architecture Biennale of Venice, 2002   Photo : Niklaus Stauss

Distortions

Philippe Rahm

The architecture of Decostered and Rahm proceeds by way of space-time distortions. We work on the very matter of space and time, using slips, shifts, accelerations and contractions. By going beyond the traditional metric and volumetric frame, our projects embrace a wish to extend the field of architecture into new dimensions. We work in the spectrum of the void and the density of the body, in the folds of time, and in the warping of distances and climates. The works proceed by way of climatic and temporal modification, generating a host of temporary local breaks, geographical breaches, astronomical shifts, and temporal contractions.

The current phenomena of globalisation and climatic irregularity accentuates the drift of man-oriented space into an autonomous space/time-frame, outside the natural astronomical and meteorological rhythms. The spaces that we occupy each day are conditioned somewhere around 21°C, at a relative humidity level of 50 per cent, with a brightness of 2000 lux, just like a fine spring day which you have decided to repeat ad infinitum, everywhere and forever and ever. This is the perpetual spring of the mythical *Ogygie* which is gradually being unfolded and elongated until it forms a global climatic continuum. A condition beyond biological cycles, which has neither sleep nor season, night nor winter, rain nor cold. The information is instant; the connection simultaneous, the network is global, and uninterrupted. Here and now, but also there and tomorrow.

Faced with this increasing and mean homogenization of space, our architecture tries to give rise to faults and flaws, meteorological dislocations, shifts of environments, and displacements, at once climatic, temporal and physiological. Our architecture works in the field of modernity, in the artificial transformation of places and climates; however we seek the supernatural rather than the artificial, the super-territorialised rather than the deterritorialised. In this sense it is architecture akin to a supermodernism.

Hormonorium Philippe Rahm and Jean-Gilles Décosterd   Photo: Jean-Michel Landecy

Swiss Pavilion, 8th Biennale of Architecture, Venice, 2002
Collaboration: Jérôme Jacqmin, Catherine Rossier, Lausanne/Elena Solari, Mestre-Venise
with Professor Urs Scherrer, Lausanne, and Dr Anna Wirz-Justice, Basel.
Submusic composed by AIR (J-B Dunckel – N. Godin),
mastered by Hervé Dutournier at Studios Translab-Paris, June 2002

Hormonorium

The Hormonorium is a sudden drop in altitude, a high altitude climate which is compressed in just a few feet onto a seaside climate, a spatial contraction of 10,000 feet on to 10 feet.

The Hormonorium was exhibited as the Swiss Pavilion at the 8th Biennale of Architecture in Venice in 2002. The design was based on the disappearance of the physical boundaries between space and the organism, as revealed by biology and the neurosciences. Going beyond visual and metric mediation, the space sought to establish continuity between the living and the non-living, opening the space up to invisible, electromagnetic and biological determinations.

While the Hormonorium created an alpine-like climate it was also an assemblage of physiological devices acting on the endocrine and neurovegetative systems. In this sense it can be viewed as a physiological representation of an alpine environment, to be ingested, through respiration, through the retina and the dermis.

The dazzling, luminous false floor was made of Plexiglas to allow the passage of UV light. It was made up of 528 fluorescent tubes, which emitted a white light that reproduces the solar spectrum, with UV-A and UV-B. Because of its inverted radiation, emitted from the ground, as in the case of snow, the luminous radiation is not blocked by the eyelids, the eyelashes or the natural tilt of the head. This very bright light of between 5000 and 10,000 lux stimulates the retina, which transmits information to the pineal gland that causes a decrease in melatonin secretion. By so lowering the level of this hormone in the body, this environment allows us to experience a decrease in fatigue, a probable increase in sexual desire, and regulation of our moods. Due to the presence of UV-A, the Hormonorium was a tanning environment, while the UV-B rays enabled the synthesis of vitamin D.

Increasing the level of nitrogen in the Hormonorium reduced the oxygen level from 21 per cent to 14.5 per cent, which is that found at altitudes of about 3000 metres. This oxygen-rarefied space causes slight hypoxia, which may initially be manifested by clinical states such as confusion, disorientation or bizarre behaviour, but also a slight euphoria due to endorphin production. After about ten minutes, there is a measurable 'natural' increase in erythropoietin (EPO) and hematocrit levels, as well as a strengthening of the cardiovascular and respiratory systems. Erythropoietin is produced by the kidneys. This protein hormone reaches the bone marrow, where it stimulates the production of red blood cells, thus increasing the supply of oxygen to the muscles. Decreasing the oxygen level therefore has a stimulating effect that may improve the body's physical capabilities by up to 10 per cent.

The Hormonorium was therefore a climate that stimulated the body physiologically, while simultaneously offering a new model for a de-contextualised, de-geographised public space. A physico-chemical place, it offered a partial displacement of a climate from higher elevations to the seaside, enhancing the body's equilibrium through regulation of the neurovegetative system. Moreover, it was a place of potential transformation of our physical performance, through stimulation, through the physiological modification of human nature. An infra-functionalist architecture, a place whose visibility expands into the upper and lower wavelengths of the light spectrum, into the invisibility of the chemical compositions of the air, an endocrine architecture, to be breathed, to be dazzled by.

Winterhouse

The Fabrice Hybert's Winterhouse is a displacement of latitude in real time from the south to the north hemisphere, like a curve of space-time, overlaying a Tahitian summer on a Vendée winter, in western France, or a summer's day on a winter's night.

This project is concerned with the invisible modification of space by modern climate control. The aim is to broaden the field of architecture to the design of the invisible, of electromagnetic fields and chemical realms. The house is to be constructed in the countryside of the Vendée, near a small river, at a distance from other dwellings. We imagine it as a winter refuge, a conditioned space that will afford protection against cold and harsh weather during the rigors of winter. Our design is intended to restore to specialist engineers the task of designing the technical aspects of the building such as heating and ventilation as architectural elements. Hence the design considers the physical material of the heating and ventilation system not merely as a secondary aspect of architecture, but as its fundamental raison d'être.

Positioned in an outdoor winter temperature of 5°C the interior of the house is climate-controlled to 20°C, with 50 per cent humidity. If modern climate control of space is abstract and invisible, we propose here to construe it as the artificial reproduction of a geographically localised, chemically determined climate. Thus, in winter the interior of the house in the Vendée becomes a meridional or a tropical climate, at the choice of the occupant. For this purpose we have developed an architecture of air, invisible but physically modified. The heating system becomes a space for the production of this air, and contains not just the technical apparatus, but also exotic plants, earth, microorganisms and mineral substances from a region of the planet where the temperature is actually 20°C, with 50 per cent humidity. These plants, through photosynthesis and their emanations, will determine the chemical quality of the air that will then be pulsed into the living space. The light in this space will be determined by the real-time reproduction of the astronomical rhythm and light intensity characteristic of the delocalised region.

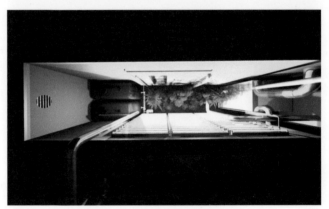

Winterhouse
Philippe Rahm and Jean-Gilles Décosterd

Collection CCI, Musée Nationale d'Art
Moderne, Beaubourg, Centre Pompidou,
France, 2002

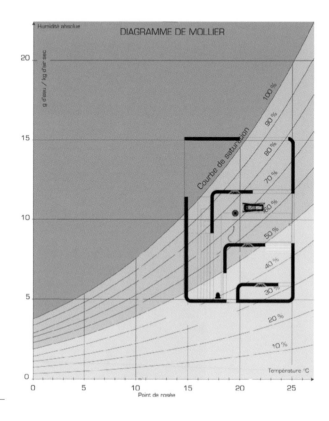

DIAGRAMME DE MOLLIER

Humidité absolue

g d'eau / kg d'air sec

Courbe de saturation

100 %
90 %
80 %
70 %
60 %
50 %
40 %
30 %
20 %
10 %

Température °C

Point de rosée

Mollier's housing, 2005

The Mollier's housing is a longitudinal contraction, by a decrease of the level of the humidity of the air from 100 per cent RH (relative humidity) to 30 per cent RH. The island of Eybesfed in Austria is a place of perpetual summer, beyond the earth's rotation around the sun, and the seasons.

This project reveals and qualifies an invisible but nevertheless obliged relation between interior space and moisture. It seeks to transform a physical problem of the building into a question of architecture, until it becomes the efficient cause of the form.

The natural breathing of the occupants and the use of hot water, are the origin of the presence of water vapour in a domestic space. A person at rest produces approximately 40 grams of water vapour per hour and up to 150 grams per hour in activity. The use of a bathroom releases up to 800 grams in 20 minutes and that of a kitchen 1500 grams per hour. The typical response to the excessive presence of the water vapour in interior space is given today by the banality of the technical systems of ventilation. We propose here to formalise space according to the water vapour itself, opening a major and complex relation between the inhabitant, their body and the space according to its physical and chemical characteristics.

Our project establishes a space stratification of the water content. In the manner of a Russian headstock the dwelling is conceived according to the renewal of air in the house, considering the relationship between the driest with wettest, the more pure with the more vitiated, the room to be slept in with the bathroom.

However the project refuses the functional programming of space according to specific activities, rather it creates more or less dry spaces and more or less wet spaces, to occupy freely, to adapt themselves according to time and seasons. The plan of the house is a spatialisation of the diagram of Mollier, creating new corresponding programming sciences, where the same space can accommodate functions a priori separate. Room 1 (drier, sauna) – 0 per cent to 30 per cent relative humidity; Room 2 (room, office) – 30 per cent to 60 per cent relative humidity; Room 3 (bathroom, kitchen) – 60 per cent to 90 per cent relative humidity; Room 4 (swimming pool, lake) – 90 per cent to 100 per cent relative humidity.

It is through the variation of the relative humidity that this architecture takes shape and formalises spaces of the dwelling, the real and carnal immersion of the body of the inhabitants in the wet and variable body of space. The building establishes new, sensual and physiological relations between the inhabitant and space. It also engages in closer links with the lake landscape of Vassivière in the Limousin. The project amplifies the hygrometrical stratification with the landscape, integrating the physical presence of the water of the lake and natural external moisture like one of the rooms of the house.

Mollier's Housing
Philippe Rahm Architects

Residences of holidays, Vassivière in the Limousin, France, 2005
Client:SYMIVA (mixed interdépartemental and regional trade union of Vassivière)
Collaborator: Jérôme Jacqmin

The Duration of Light Project 1   David Thomas

Duration

David Thomas

Painting has a very specific position and function in our culture, although recently it has been seen by some as a disintegrating superpower hanging on to a crumbling empire, as an end rather than a means, as content rather than a tool. This approach leads to limited ideas about what painting is, let alone what could constitute a relevant contemporary painting practice. It is useful to remember here that painting is not a homogeneous entity. Painting by its very nature is a complexity, a multiplicity, operating in the world as ideas and actions, as phenomena and language.

Painting remains important because in certain of its manifestations it enables us to become aware of how we perceive, construct meaning and experience. It is a model for thinking, questioning, representing, feeling and understanding our world. It intertwines our internal and the external experiences of the world in actual and virtual forms.

Elisabeth Grosz in her essay 'The future of space toward an architecture of invention'[1] argues for a concept of the logic of invention, which she opposes to the Aristotelian logic of identity, reflection, reason and self-containment. (She claims that a logic of invention still has to be invented, while I would suggest it already exists via the model of art). She suggests:

> Only such a logic can mediate between the reflective categories of philosophical thought and the pragmatic requirements of an empirical object. Instead of the self containment of the syllogism (in which conclusions are logically entailed in validly constituted premises), a logic of invention is necessarily expansive, ramifying and expedient, producing not premises so much as techniques, not conclusions so much as solutions, not arguments so much as effects.

Grosz continues: 'Architecture too is bound up with problem solving and with multiplicities, though the multiplicities with which it deals are not simply conceptual or simply material.'[2] It is in this context I will discuss certain ideas that have affected my practice particularly regarding painting/installation, that is a painting extended in time and space, which by its very nature is hybridised, relational, existing amid the world.

The Duration of Light Project 1   David Thomas

The thought of Henri Bergson provided a useful model for the consideration of duration, of the actual and the virtual and of the composite. His is a philosophy and method in sympathy with the holistic nature of research in the visual arts rooted in concrete experience in the continuum of time embodied in a living being. Bergson called this continuum of experiencing, duration (durée). I am interested how this temporal field of duration can be used to affect the understanding, delivery and nature of content in painting and painting/installation. Bergson's use of the term is at once specific and complex, understanding duration as consisting of many durations.[3] Temporal awareness is not just an instant or a stretch of time but an unfolding of various rhythms, layers or pulses; it is a complexity, a continuum in which change occurs, is recognised, and in which movement exists. 'Temporal structure is not a matter of putting together given discrete items. On the contrary, so called discrete items are only apparent when we have a need to pluck them from our continuing experience.'[4]

Implications exist here for both content and form, for the producer and receiver of content, for memory and perception, and for understanding the nature of dynamic structure and composition in painting as well as in installation. Readings exist for the viewer to select, which in turn affect other readings that highlight that content is in the process of becoming.

In Bergson's understanding of duration, there are actual and virtual durations. There is the duration of matter: the actual, measurable and fixed, and our own duration: virtual, internal and moving. They are different forms of knowledge, one fixed, the other in movement. It is as result of this, that we have, the pulse or the rhythm.[5] Bergson makes a distinction between intuition and intellect. The measurable world of space is actual, manifest as complexities external to the perceiver, and understood by the intellect as an abstract representation, an idea and therefore fixed, separating the brain, body and the world.

Virtual duration is a temporal experience recognised through intuition. It is an ongoing embodied experience of time, internal and ongoing in our life, a continuum. It is how we experience the world and is absolute.[6] Our experience of reality is therefore a composite where the internal and the external or the actual and the virtual meet. A composite is a mixture of things different in kind: experience gives us a composite of space and duration.[7]

For Bergson, it is not a matter of opposing these as a dualism or reducing the multiple to one, but of distinguishing between the two types of multiplicity. He wrote: 'When sitting on the bank of a river, the flowing of the water, or the gliding of a bird, the uninterrupted murmur of deep life, are for us three different things or a single one, at will'.[8] Perception here operates as action, not only representation in the duration of time. Memory informs perception and operates to bring the past into the present, the virtual moves into the actual, as a mixture of experience and representation: a composite.

I have used the ideas of the composite and multiplicity to assist with the development of art works that reconcile, not unify differences of kind. Artworks are composites where diverse languages and sensation meet in concrete form. The internal and external meet in the actual time and space of the present, in the experience of the viewer.

My recent works explore the intersection of painting and the world, often extending the pictorial space of painting into the actual space of installation, creating fields for the viewer to reflect upon and project upon, where contents become recoverable in the experience of negotiating the work over time. The works exploit time and duration in order to create 'slow works' asserting a contemplative function for art.

By describing the two projects *Duration of Light Project* 2004 and *The Black Reflection Photopaintings* 2001-3, I can perhaps suggest the complexity of experiencing the work, as an eye in a feeling, thinking body amid time and space, amid culture. The distribution of signifiers in time and space means that content is recovered as the viewer moves through the work. The site of the work is recognised as carrying readings. The body operates amid it, inserted into the work through devices such as reflection, colour saturation, placement and interval.

In *The Duration of Light Project 1*, I created a reflection work by painting a large black acrylic rectangle to the external face of the glass wall of Project Space, RMIT. When viewed from the inside this appeared as a mirror. The viewers saw themselves perceiving in a space, amid a bigger space and time, their reflections framed by external views, inside meeting outside. From the exterior the black form blocked views of the interior, deferring readings and creating formal tonal contrasts.

Within the gallery the rectangular monochrome wall paintings referenced colours observable through the windows, setting up relational comparisons between the changeable and the fixed, the constructed and the actual, between here and there, now and then. Next door, the small Spare Room space was painted intense yellow, creating an immersive environment affecting the viewers' perception of colours and light, heightening the relative nature of perception.

The Black Reflection Photopaintings   David Thomas

The Black Reflection Photopaintings 2001-3, are photographs on which gloss enamel rectangles are painted leaving the edge of the photographs visible, similar to the black window painting/installation discussed above. They are composites existing between the representational conventions of photography and the actuality of painting. What photographs are as well as what they are of, is important. Photography is presented as another form of representation, not as a privileged realism or truth. The photograph is an image of an event, a memory, another time another place. It also functions as a physical support. The material and temporal nature of the photograph is highlighted, contrasting with the properties of the enamel paint.

The painted black monochrome rectangle initially functions to obscure the information behind it, asking the viewer to examine the periphery of the work, generating readings and associations from fact to symbol. The paint surface contains dust which is not only symbolic but which also addresses scale. The physical matter and gesture of the paint reveals its application in time. The black gloss paint reflects real space/time/events/people, referencing the traditional mimetic space of 'Western realist' painting and a 'live time' screen.

Here the viewers see themselves observing in the present. The works are sites for becoming aware of our changing perceptions and constructions of meanings. Again meanings here are relational, informed by context, related to our attention and intention, that is, what we are looking for and how we look for it within the continuum of time.

1   See Elizabeth Grosz, 'The future of space toward an architecture of invention', cited
    in Weibel Peter, ed, *Olafur Eliasson: Surroundings Surrounded. Essays on Space and
    Science*, Karlsruhe, Cambridge Massachusetts and London: Neue Galerie Graz, ZKM
    and MIT Press, 2000, 254-55.

2   ibid, 255.

3   Henri Bergson, *Matter and Memory*, 1911, trans. Nancy Margaret Paul and W Scott
    Palmer, London: Muirhead Library of Philosophy, Harvester Press, 1978, 342.

4   F C T Moore, *Bergson: Thinking Backwards*, New York: Cambridge University Press,
    1996, 55.

5   Gilles Deleuze, *Bergsonism*, New York: Zone Books,1997, 'Intuition as a method',
    13-35.

6   Paul Crowther on intuition in *The Language of Twentieth-Century Art. A Conceptual
    History*, New Haven and London: Yale University Press, 1997, 5.

7   Gilles Deleuze in *Bergsonism*, 37.

The Black Reflection Photopaintings – Paris at Night   David Thomas

Looking Practice 8: Corner Study Linda Choi

The Return Megan Evans

Slips, Shifts and Reversals

Patricia Pringle

According to one theory of conjuring, the feats which induce a sense of magical experience can be divided into a relatively small number of categories. These include *productions* (from not being to being), *disappearances* (from being to not being), *transformations* (from being in this way to being in that), *transpositions* (from being here to being) and *natural science laws disobeyed* (which is in itself one definition of magic).

A group of emerging artists and designers, whose work deals with the experience of perception, were invited to create works to direct attention to such shifts, slips and reversals within the spaces of Melbourne's Conical Gallery.

To walk round the exhibition was to experience an exercise circuit of perceptions, heightening awareness of one's own perceiving body in action. Many of the works manipulated the audience physically by inviting participation in their performance – stepping up, leaning closer, throwing the head back – while at the same time heightening our awareness of acts of looking, seeing and speculating.

Several of the works were called into existence through the engagement of the viewer entering their zone. As spaces and relationships were revealed, they became cohesive spaces for the duration of the experience, visible only to their occupant and falling back into their disparate elements once the attention was withdrawn. In particular *Slipping Spaces* (Olivia and Madeleine Griffith) and *The Return* (Megg Evans) each brought us into a tantalising relationship with our own self, one where our reflection looked not back at us but onwards to another place. The Griffiths' work, which used a video loop to let viewers see themselves in an enchanted other world, drew on the bright and dark enticements of fairytale, heightened by its placement in a secretive understair position at child's-eye level. In contrast Megg Evans' unsettling endless mirror circuit called up the relentless displacements of phobia, filled with paradox and prohibition, by refusing ever to let us reach the person that we were following, who was again our own self.

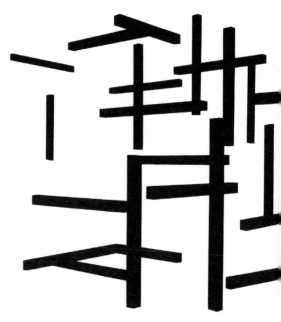

Sanne Mestrom's large work *The Myth of Political Vision* used 3D techniques and stereoscopic lenses to focus on the process of perception and the revelation of multilayered realities through shifts in vision. The sensation of perception was visceral; one felt the machinery of vision in action. The dubious grandiosity that its scale implied sat nicely against Tim Mattison's *Tremor*, which in contrast conjured an equally post-apocalyptic narrative out of simple scraps of cardboard and torn paper. These were used to create a stop-motion video epic whose fluttering protagonist, animated out of the most ephemeral media, rose up for a short moment of glory before being once more dismembered and reduced to fragments. Viewers found ourselves engaging with the epic even as they laughed at the incongruity of it all, their own physicality perhaps briefly troubled by an empathetic embodiment with the flat and tattered figure as it shifted from animated humanoid to non-existence.

The Myth of Political Vision Sanne Mestrom

Works by Linda Choi and Rowena Martinich brought viewers emphatically back to their own bodies. These again set us in motion. In *Looking Practice 8: Corner Study* Linda Choi set up an experience against which it was almost impossible to stand still for long, so

Tremor
Tim Mattison

Slipping Spaces
Olivia & Madeleine Griffith

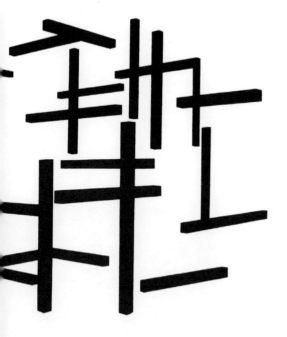

compelling was the desire to move from one position to another to relish the optical quandary that it provoked. In an acute-angled corner space she had positioned a full size photograph of the corner itself, imposing a picture plane and intercepting the visual continuum. As one moved in and out of the zone in which the photographic simulation matched the context of the viewing space, the walls forming the acute angle seemed to swing round in an attempt to sustain some possible view.

Rowena Martinich made us move also, but with a meditative pace. There was no single position from which to see her pieces which, like landscape, were scanned with the physical eye and the mental eye. They made the viewer hover, while looking up, looking through and looking past with a swelling and contracting of vision.

With *Reflection: Spatial Screening* Erin O'Callaghan shifted time with an illusory reflection. Viewers glancing towards an existing window would see the reflection of the space that they were in but at a different moment in time, and being moved through by other gallery visitors. The disconcerting effect of this was that one felt the presence of other invisible visitors in one gallery while oneself becoming an invisible occupant of that other gallery. This was achieved by back-projecting video on to the window/screen via apparatus which was concealed in a purpose-built chamber attached to the outside of the gallery wall.

The physical scale of the behind-the-scenes construction necessary to make this exhibit function flawlessly made the delicacy of the final exhibit all the more touching. Hannah Bertram's two small works, *Echo* and *echo*, demonstrated the power of small things to work on us physically, calling us to move closer, engaging the magnifying eye of our attention. Lacellike traceries of powdery colour, they suggested that the molecules of wall and floor had slowly and quietly changed places. Scarcely visible at first sight, they grew in the mind to become substantial works which would be called up in memory long after their delicate placement and displacements of dust and wall had vanished.

Reflection: Spatial Screening
Erin O'Callaghan

Echo and echo
Hannah Bertram

Wingbeat/Moss Glass Janet Laurence

Glasshouse

Janet Laurence

The Glasshouse series of works interface with architecture and landscape to create elemental, immersive and enmeshed spaces where the language of porosity and fluidity is used to create a fusion with the environment, slowed spaces that are reflective, to bring us into contact with the life-world. An in-between space, where fixity of meaning becomes fugitive, enabling notions of transcience and transformation to be invoked.

The Green between Glass is a large glass veil between the restaurant and the foyer of a Melbourne Hotel. It is a visually fluid wall shifting between transparency, translucency and opacity, the material and the immaterial, encapsulating images of the edible plant world.

The wall is made up of overlapping glass panels. Layers of green glazes have been poured onto the glass, possibly with the gesture of sowing seeds forming these 'spilt' fluids, whose 'flowing' presence suggests the essential oils and liquids we extract from plants.

In varying degrees of transparency these fluid panels underlay and overlay screen-printed drawings from early botanical illustrations of medicinal herbs and plants. The plants' Latin and common names are interwoven to form horizontal bands of text through the centre and bottom of the glass panels. Like large-scale vertical microscope slides we are able to inspect at close range the liquids and solids, the chemistry encapsulated within the layers of glass.

Both transparent and membranous this elusive glass wall shifting in light attracts us from a distance with its abstract fluid green, as a wall of light. It is continually within the present reflecting the light world around it whilst creating glimpses through from one side to the other. It can be viewed from both sides, each offering a different aspect. The elusive layering both obscures and distils our vision, suggesting the facts about plants whilst at the same time conjuring the ephemeral, fleeting and fluid nature of organic matter and of light and glass itself.

As a botanical frieze, the artwork combines the graphic representation of edible herbal matter with the notion of its immateriality its ability to decay, decompose, be ingested, distilled to extract essential flavours and elixirs both static and fluid reminding us of the transformative fluxus of nature. It is a poetic foray into the vegetal world where flavour, essence, and the fundamental chemistry of medicinal herbs are frozen within glass.

The *Verdant Works* are an exploration of reflected and veiled environments of the physical world. They allow one to engage with a way of looking within the world rather than at it and invite the viewer to experience oneself through materiality. It is also very much a space that one reflects oneself onto it and become a reflective space. 'Many of the works hark back to Laurence's earlier expressions of elemental and alchemical states. The glass is presented as a clear fluid, a medium which can suspend or transmute molecules of matter or traces of a reflection.'[1]

In works such as *Wingbeat/Moss Glass (2004)* a sense of uncertainty and dissolution is induced by the overlapping images of the modernist architecture and the adjacent forest. 'The dualities of nature and culture have become diffused and entangled through the play of multiple reflections and the seeping interference of sulphurous, unguent swirls of pigment.'[2]

In *Space Dissolving*, the work shows the iconic Barcelona pavilion of Mies van der Rohe transforming through the layering of glass panels as fluid and organic forms appearing to dissolve it which brings to mind Toyo Ito writings on it:

> The Mies pavilion in Barcelona ... a space filled with such 'fluidity'. This combination of steel, glass and stone does not, nonetheless, imply the hardness of these materials. Glazing and stones are merely the flat and simple planar components of the space. Spaces created by the combination of horizontally extending abstract planes have an infinite expanse ... the mutual intrusion of inside and outside spaces ... the sensation ... lightness of flowing air ... thickness of molten liquid.

Verdant in Solids   Janet Laurence

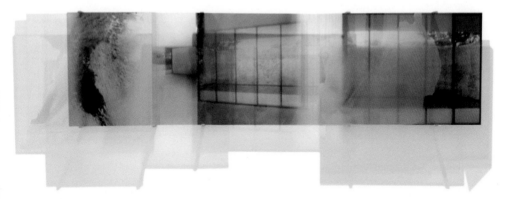

Space Dissolving   Janet Laurence

...What we experience here is not the flow of air but the sense of wandering and drifting gently underwater. This very sensation makes the space distinct and unique.

...This fluidity and density felt in the Barcelona Pavilion gradually disappeared even from Mies's own architecture. Instead, architectural formality rapidly gained its place. That space which once felt fluid was lost, as if liquid had been transformed into solid. And, as we await the 21st century, we are once again in search of that erotic architecture that fuses with the environment.[3]

All these works are made up of veils of varying degrees of transparency, both in order for their matter to be experienced and to create a degree of difficulty in seeing, to draw us in to immerse us and yet the material of glass itself reflects us back as Michael Tawa has said:

To gloss-over is to skim, scan, slide-over – so as to miss engaging or connecting with something. The slipperiness of glass is not only in its glossy surface, but also in its internal propensity to slide, its fluidic constitution. The slippage it effects is also in its betrayal of transparency – its mineral lineage. Glass is neither a liquid or a solid. In its deferral of distinctions between stability and movement, between inside and outside, glass slips from being seen through, to being looked at, to itself looking and throwing glances. Towards what? Towards us, as a measure of its appearance, as a turning towards existentiation.[4]

Elixir is a site-specific permanent artwork that forms part of the 'necklace' of art, architectural and landscape projects that are transforming the mountainous traditional rice farming community and its spectacular landscape with its radical seasonal changes in Echigo Tsumari, Nigata Prefecture, Japan.

One makes a pilgrimage to this place, and a journey to Echigo-Tsumari is a journey to the *Snow Country* of Kawabata's 1948 novel:

> In the depths of the mirror, the evening landscape moved by, the mirror and the reflected figures like motion pictures superimposed one on the other. The figures and the background were unrelated, and the figures, transparent and intangible, and the background, dim in the gathering darkness, melted into a sort of symbolic world not of this world.[5]

The Echigo Tsumari Triennale is a visionary project under the directorship of Fram Kitagawa and Art Front. It is regarded as the major event in the Japanese contemporary art calendar whilst at the same time managing to involve the local community to both realise and then maintain the projects. This is a great experiment where art becomes the bridge between humanity and nature.

The region, spread out over a vast area, is regenerated by this contemporary cultural event and interventions, many of which are permanent. There is a wonderful variety of sites through the different villages, towns and landscapes.

Art projects are commissioned every three years by a vast range of internationally well known artists such as Christian Boltanski, Magdalena Jetelova and Yayoi Kasuma. as well as younger Japanese artists. As the boundaries between architecture and art are increasingly blurred, here the interweaving is with the environment itself, as a reference and a framing, resulting in a successful synthesis that reinforces a respect for the natural environment.

Recently two major architectural projects were commissioned, one being the No Butai Cultural Centre by MRDV from the Netherlands, a white building that disappears in the deep snow winters. In a nearby area wrapping around a forest is the Museum of Natural Science, a red rust cor-ten steel bunkered into the landscape, designed by architects Takaharu and Yui Tezuka.

The surrounding forests are woven pathways lined with story stones by Jenny Holtzer and Kawamata's wooden walkways and shelters creating trajectories and spaces for one to experience and inhabit the landscape.

One may chose to spend a night at the James Turrell *House of Light*, a house designed by Tadao Ando, in which one experiences the series of spaces of disclosed light and others that open and close to reveal the transforming aspects of light and colour of day into night and night into day.

Another night could be spent in the *Dream House* by Marina Abramovic, offering visitors the experience of sleeping in suits and sarcophagi (sleeping boxes) with dream-enhancing magnets and mineral stones, in rooms coloured by their old glass sliding screens. It is a traditional wooden farmhouse transformed into a psychic space.

Within the garden is the *Elixir House*, a restored, traditional, small, wood storage house. The interior within the dark wood house is transformed into a light reflecting glass laboratory like space echoing both an old apothecary, and tiny, botanical museum. It is an experiential space that immerses one into the essence of the surrounding landscape.

This wooden interior room of *Elixir* is lined and layered with glass veils stained with plant fluids, and inscribed with the plant names, botanical drawings and medicinal remedies from this environment (sourced from ancient books and individuals within the region). Around the edge are hanging, elongated blown glass vials each containing plant specimens.

In the centre of the room is a layered cantilevered glass bench laden with glass laboratory vessels filled with the elixirs: extracts of plants mixed with shochu as potions/drinks, which one takes from tiny glass beakers. A glass box containing the clear fluid shochu sits above, casting light reflections around the space playing out the Japanese poetic of light from shadow.

The work reveals and regenerates an ancient tradition and knowledge of the medicinal plants whilst forming an intimacy with the natural surrounding landscape.

1   Freya Lombardo, 'Verdant works', *Artichoke*, 08/02, 2004.
2   Sally Couacaud, catalogue essay for *After Nature* exhibition, Lake Macquarie Gallery, 2003.
3   Toyo Ito, 'Tarzans in the media forest', *2G* 2, 1997.
4   Michael Tawa, 'On Glass', Z Glass Conference, Sydney College of the Arts, 1997.
5   Yasunari Kawabata, *Snow Country*, translator Edward G Seidensticker, New York: Vintage International, 1948; as quoted by Drusilla Modjeska in *The Green in the Glass: The Art of Janet Laurence*, Sydney: Pesaro Press, 2006.

Three-Dimensional Photography Installation   Erin O'Callaghan

media

Perspective Corrections

Ian de Gruchy

I started my practice of projection twenty-five years ago, working with club and gallery spaces and theatre performances as a way to present my artwork. In the early days I was experimenting with image, ideas, content and technology to do with projection. I was interested in twisting the process of projection itself, playing with the distortions that the projected image made possible and the potentials of scattering projections around and through a space. The work I am doing now uses those same techniques, but turns it on itself, in order to understand what this notion of distortion is, and somehow reinvent it.

I have moved from the idea of scatter and distortion to the idea of very deliberate control of image and perspectives and have got to the point where I am building my own cameras and using different digital technologies so that I may document what the potential distortions of the projections might be and then fit them back into a process of understanding space.

When I first began to work on public projections I understood how to vaguely project things into walls, but the unpredictability of how these things actually operate started to annoy me. So I realised I had to begin to plot the entire site and once that plot was done then I would have a rough idea of what that projection was going to do on whatever I was projecting upon.

Eventually I built a camera which I call a cine projector camera, a camera obscura. What I can do now is take the lens that I think is going to be appropriate for the job and put it on this camera and position the camera in what I think is roughly the best place to put the projectors and take a picture so that I have a perfect rendering of whatever the projection is going to do on the building. I can then take the picture into my computer and rework the perspectives according to a grid and distort the proposed projected images to exactly the angle of the projection. What it means is that I can now take on just about any space and resolve the ideas exactly into the building.

The development of this process led me on to working with Barbara Kruger on a series of projects that have been done all over the world in a number of architectural configurations and using from nine projectors to twenty projectors. These projects involved the calculation of perspective distortion, how to get the projectors into the ceiling and out of the gallery space and programming the work so that it acted like a clock and didn't have to be turned on and off and reset, as the works would sometimes run for two months. What interested me was the complete sense of the installation, architecturally wrapping the entire space including the floor, how three projected images would make up one image on a wall and how the projections could be negotiated around the building's columns.

Recently I installed projections at three sites simultaneously for the Perth Festival: at Barrack Arch at the top of King Georges Terrace, at His Majesty's Theatre and at the Duxton Hotel. Public building projects such as these offer the opportunity to play with site and memory. The terrace had been entirely stripped of historical buildings so the projection became the opportunity to put one back into it. With His Majesty's Theatre, which had had its original verandahs removed, I used four projectors on angles from the awnings of buildings across the road which worked together to fit the original façade verandah detail back onto the building. The Duxton Hotel offered the opportunity to create a sixty-metre-tall, twenty-eight image show based on the theme of migration.

I like the idea of taking on the side of the building and creating a new façade out of it. With these new techniques it means that instead of it being a happenstance notion of projection onto the buildings surface I can actually start to sculpt the projected images into the building's fabric and history.

Barrack Arch Projection Ian De Gruchy

His Majesty's Theatre Projection Ian De Gruchy

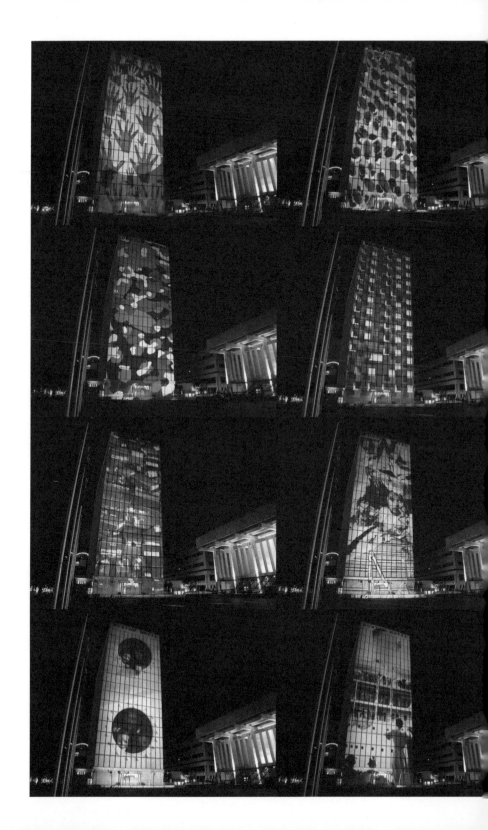

Duxton Hotel Projection Ian De Gruchy

The Video Effect

Sonia Leber and Ramesh Ayyar

How does video technology influence how we see, hear and imagine architecture and the built environment? Until recently, the ease of mechanical reproduction in photography made it a key tool in representing architecture and the built environment. Within a suspended moment, architecture was frozen as a balanced composition: fixed, static and silent.

Video Effect

The Video Effect: Marsella Christine, Romy Handley, Meyliza Kotama, Michael Gadise, Mel Pimolsook, Djena Cero, Alissa Caplan, Toby Dodson and Debbie Minter

Video's gift to the architect is the gift of articulating time. Space can be shown to change; it can be rendered as flux in a series of changing relationships. We can examine the qualities of a space: the similarities and the disjunctions, the proximities and distances, the calm and the vertiginous. Space can be revealed as a multiplicity of unfolding journeys; a series of performed architectural events that invite us to enter.

With video, the sound environment is made audible. Soundscapes reveal the changing acoustic qualities of a space, registering changes in volumes, surfaces and materials. Other sounds, real or imagined, start to emerge from in situ or outside recordings.

Editing further complicates the mix. Sounds and images – at first observational and phenomenological – can be fragmented and re-configured into the analytical, the cultural and the imaginary. Essays can be constructed in image and sound, without recourse to language.

The works produced by RMIT Interior Design students for the exhibition at the BUS gallery as part of the Sensoria Festival, recognised that video is more than a tool of representation. Video influences our spatial acuity, affecting both how we remember and design the built environment. The more ephemeral of experiences – the play of light in a stairwell, a wall of shimmering reflections – can be captured and explored.

Video allows some spaces to materialise as a series of disjunctive fragments, in a montage of changing perspectives. Other spaces are able to reveal themselves more slowly as tableaux vivants. In these spaces of contemplation, the restrained, minute occurrences captured on video take on great significance.

The Video Effect: Solédad Herrera, Jakob Lange and Joanne Morris

Manifest

Christopher Kaltenbach and Ross McLeod

As the centrepiece for the Sensoria conference, Christopher Kaltenbach and
Erin O'Callaghan led a team of students from the RMIT Interior Design program,
working together with local and international artists and designers to create the
sensorial event, Manifest. For one evening only, the pristine gallery spaces of
the Australian Centre for Contemporary Art were transformed into a carnivale of
sensuous experiences.

The event was developed as a series of spatial conditions that not only sought to
challenge our understanding of sensory space but questioned the role designers
play in addressing political and social issues. The evening's spatial and sensorial
events were generated by a set of ideas which considered the issues of childhood
and the loss of innocence, refugees, population density, cultural interaction
and identity.

Foyer Space, Manifest Event, Australian Centre for Contemporary Art

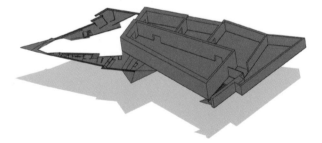

As you entered the foyer you were tempted by a range of gastronomic oddities prepared by chef George Caloumbaris. His approach to food takes on notions and tastes from childhood to produce delicacies that are both familiar and confronting. His cooking experiments with ingredients and ideas, in order to challenge the perception of 'culinary correctness'. Using his 'molecular gastronomy' technique Caloumbaris juxtaposes sweet and salty, hot and cold, aroma and texture within extraordinary presentations which make us aware of the boundaries and potentials of our sense of taste.

Working in front of the crowd as a live performance the chef offered a number of sample dishes which were produced through the unusual blending of jellies, binding and freezing techniques and carbonate processes. The offerings included frozen lemon and salt lollypops, peanut butter and jam chocolate bars, spoons of gin and tonic jelly with champagne foam and delicate meringues cooked by freezing in liquid nitrogen. This was food beyond sustenance, it was food presented as experience, as design, as art.

In the far corner of the foyer a platoon of trained barmen served a variety of 42 Below Feijoa Vodka cocktails mixed with fresh cucumber and Chi Herbal mineral water. The bar area was illuminated by the Zumtobel Staff Active Light wall system, which emitted a uniform glow of continuous blends of colour throughout the evening.

Moving from the foyer space into the first of the four galleries the viewer was confronted with a flotilla of helium-filled red lifesavers floating within a deeply hued dark blue haze. The balloons, made by Christopher Langton and Peter Knights, were tethered to concrete tiles designed by Mijeong Lee which had been subtly printed with the faces of babies, seemingly staring up at the floating lifesavers through the lighting effects created by Daniel Zika. The seams of these concrete lily pads as well as the perimeter of the gallery were embedded with lengths of red flexi-light which intensified and defined the installation's presence in the room. The concept of the room was concerned with how Australia deals with refugee children. The ghostly images of the babies and the surreal movements of the balloons in the blue environment meant to create a strong metaphor of the Child Overboard Scandal.

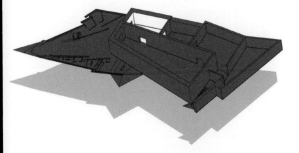

In the middle space one was immersed in a video projection and sound scape that reacted to the presence of people in the room. In response to the City of Melbourne's 2030 plan for dealing with the effects of a drastically increased population within Melbourne's central urban districts, the space attempted to demonstrate how density could bring calming effects to an environment. When the room filled with people the projected imagery and ambient sounds became slower and quieter. As the room emptied the imagery would become faster and the sound louder.

To assist in achieving the respondent environment controlled by the continuous flows of visitors Jeremy Yuille and Gregory More worked with Soledad Herrara in generating a montage of sounds and images as well as developing an application for the motion sensors. Andre Ebella from the Tokyo office of Belgium sensor company BEA coordinated the sponsorship of the motion sensors. These were used to activate the decrease or increase of media into the room.

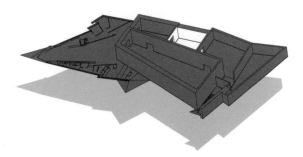

Gallery Two, Manifest Event, Australian Centre for Contemporary Art

In the corner gallery a stack of laser cut plywood sheets were piled high in the middle of the room. Amidst the backdrop of music by DJ Dom a.k.a. Goldfinger and a wash of pink light by Daniel Zika the audience were encouraged to pull down a sheet of plywood and assemble a stool to sit on. As the evening wore on over 200 people had gathered in this meeting space and many interactions and structures were built in the room.

The Zaishu stools were developed by designer Matthew Butler who, with students Kate Jackson and Jenny Ford, worked on developing a range of furniture for the event. Butler devised a design that would utilise an inexpensive material and be easily manufactured, as well as be a significant solution for the need of simple portable furniture that recycles material. The five-piece flat pack seat/table/box is made from non-precious plywood salvaged from construction sites, which is then painted and laser cut with the chair's pattern.

The painting project was art directed and curated by Andrew Mac of Citylights and the project involved twenty-five street artists who in one weekend in a laneway in Melbourne stencilled an array of images, prints and motifs onto the plywood, transporting the language of the city wall to an intimate piece of furniture in a gallery space.

Since the Manifest event, Matthew Butler has taken the project to Japan, Seoul, Milan, Sydney, Melbourne and Stockholm, and in 2006 will work with artists in India, Berlin, Sweden and New Zealand. The Zaishu project has evolved into a vibrant platform for cultural exchange, community strengthening and economic sustenance.

City Lights artists included Amac, Bleek, David Campbell, Dens, Dlux, E3, Micheal Fikaris, Tom Gerrard, HaHa, Ash Keating, LTMP, Kiernan Mangan, Monkey, Aaron O'Donnel, Pandarosa, Phibs, Prism, Reach, Reks, Rone, SRX and Vexta.

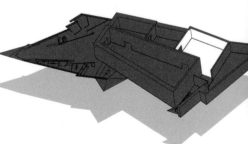

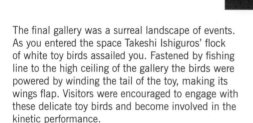

The final gallery was a surreal landscape of events. As you entered the space Takeshi Ishiguros' flock of white toy birds assailed you. Fastened by fishing line to the high ceiling of the gallery the birds were powered by winding the tail of the toy, making its wings flap. Visitors were encouraged to engage with these delicate toy birds and become involved in the kinetic performance.

The Scanner Projector installation by Gregory More graced the vast hall of the gallery. The animation required a track device for moving the projector along the thirty-one metre length of the gallery. The combination of digital video camera and laptop was self-propelled over a track placed on the floor against the length of one of the walls. The video imagery of the gallery fed into the camera in real time and was immediately processed through a time delay distortion filter developed by More. The resulting effect was a compelling slow motion feedback loop replaying and moving across the space. The strange horizontal light cut across the space in regular intervals. Silhouetted against the low pass of the projector's light Mi Kyong Lee's beanbag forms dotted the terrain, their irregularity in heights providing people with different vantage points to experience the room.

Dwarfing the doorway at the exit of the gallery space, two giant crimson pillows, made by Christopher Langton, nestled generously together. Inside this glowing canyon groups of people gathered in intimate huddles, the curvaceous forms and soft light encouraged a friendly intimacy, providing a last sensuous encounter.

Back in the foyer with a piece of experimental food in one hand and a vodka cocktail in the other, the conversation continued.

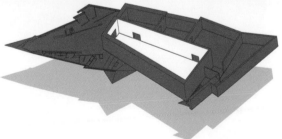

Manifest Studio: Sebastian Agricol, James Carey, Sun-Young Cho, Elena Critchley, Jenny Ford, Soledad Herrera, Kate Jackson, Raphael Kilpatrick, Mi Kyung Kim, Peter Knights, Meijong Lee, Christine Lilley and Adam Paikos.

All photos courtesy of Christopher Kaltenbach and Manifest Studio

Melbourne Interiors

Roger Kemp

The Croft Institute, a small bar located at the end of one of Melbourne's network of laneways, was the late night venue at the Sensoria Festival for an exhibition of projected video images, produced by RMIT Interior Design undergraduate students, which captured the shifting qualities of particular interior spaces in Melbourne.

Static video footage projected onto screens located in the bar presented what at first seemed like a still image; however on further observation they gave a more temporal representation of these spaces. Changes in lighting conditions and the presence of occupants moving in and out of the frame gave these images a quality of surveillance. The spaces documented included Melbourne City Watch House, Windsor Station Café, Parliament House, the State Library of Victoria, the stage set of television drama series 'Stingers' and the hairdressing salon Doctor Follicles and thirty different living rooms in Melbourne.

The occupation and inhabitation of space was a central concern for these works. Interior spaces are so often in a state of flux – ever changing, mutating and transforming. Their significance is not based on static monumentalism but rather on a lived and remembered presence. In this sense the event itself was seen as an addition to the accretion of memories associated with the Croft Institute and the images encountered on the night were reproduced as badges which visitors could souvenir as part of the experience.

This event was one of a series of exhibitions of images and texts which have been held in spaces around Melbourne over the past three years. This work sits under the title of 'Melbourne Interiors', an ongoing research project conducted by students of the Interior Design program at RMIT University.

The project seeks to select, collect and document interior spaces of Melbourne. The nature of this collection reveals and develops new imaginings and understandings of interior space, interior spaces that may be living, lived, remembered or perhaps lost.

Melbourne Interiors Badges
Croft Institute, Melbourne

Melbourne Interiors – Croft Institute:
Roger Kemp, Olivia Griffith, Alicia Remnant, Millie Cattlin,
Alex Doughty, Amber Stewart, Ting Sun, Kate Willemsen,
Sophie Whittakers

Materiamatics

Michael Trudgeon

'The best way to predict the future is to invent it.'[1]

Societies need to plan for the future in order to survive. Those that have not have perished. One is either made subservient by the future or part of its planning and making. The following comments on materials are made in this light.

Ezio Manzini, the Italian architect and writer, tells us that in the age of plastic, material certainty has vanished.[2] Wood is not wood (it might be dust and glue), stone is not stone (it might be glass and polyurethane). Materials are now what we choose to make them. In the plastic age the designer is faced with designing the materials as much as the objects, the space or the building constructed from the material. The material's performance, thermal properties, opacity and electrical conductivity, and now informational conductivity are all designable, malleable and changeable. You get to choose. While much of this research was originally restricted to the car industry and military research, the effects are now widely apparent. Given this fluid set of options the materials we select or design can truly reflect our intent. They are no longer guides or boundaries but vectors or agents of the design.

Following this assertion it could be claimed that the world of materials has two sides, one an immanent (indwelling, inherent, permanently pervading the universe, from the Latin manere, to remain), the other side, transcendent: materials in the service of ideas. This second one sees the skin as both the starting point for the experience and the possible communication of ideas (as the structure is either incidental or just expedient) and of the greatest significance.

The immanent is the world of structure and material presence; the other is a world of signs, vectors and shape shifters, a world of information. Modernism has been proposed as a kind of nude architecture or design, preoccupied with the structural notions of materials and its simple meaning, divested of any polychromatic membrane it might have had thrown over its body. My interest lies in that membrane.

To discuss materials in this light I will begin with a story of materialisation and symbiosis: the story of the bureau. We think today of a bureau as a building or department or agency occupying a building or perhaps more traditionally, a writing desk with drawers. In modern usage the French origins of the word refer not in fact to the desk but its green baize covering: an applied fabric skin. Prior to that bureau referred to a particular cloth that was thrown over a desk to signify a site for business transactions.[3] A material used to circumscribe a territory or site as fit for a specific activity or ritual. While the earlier Roman origins of the word mean bright red, the bureau has another ancestor. The rug or carpet set upon the ground in Arabic cultures is to create an environment suitable for business, one that tells others that a meeting is in progress and one that can be moved with the passage of the day's shadows to avoid the blistering direct sunlight. Here we have a material that is magic. It appears immanent; a tightly woven cloth, yet it is something else altogether: it is territory, the territory of ideas, culture and information.

In the early 1800s, the German architect and anthropologist, Gottfried Semper, while studying the classical remains of ancient Greece, discovered that they were in fact not originally monochromatic marble but painted in bright colours. For Semper the material surface realises the architecture or the design. His model of design is that of originating as an ornamental textile. In the search for authority the Italian Renaissance architect Alberti placed the origin of architecture as being constructed naked and later dressed with ornament, whereas Gottfried Semper transformed this account into one in which architecture began with the placement of textile ornament, followed by solid structure. Locating architecture as a textile art in which seamed-together textile walls envelop and wrap to give spatial enclosure, Semper suggests that architecture turns out to be nothing more than texture.[4] Semper also notes that the woven surface was first conceived as a means to separate inner life from outer and concerns the formal creation of the idea of space. That is, the wall that secures spatial enclosure has nothing directly to do with space and the division of space and that this conception of surface as abstraction precedes the wall as physical entity.

This connection between material appearance and implicate order surfaces in other concepts dating from antiquity. The Greek noun *kosmos* derives from the verb which means to order, to arrange. Thus a *kosmos* is an orderly arrangement. Moreover it is a beautiful arrangement. It is also the root of cosmetic, something which beautifies and is pleasant to look at. The cosmos is both elegant and orderly.

The significance of surface is also embedded biologically. Vilayanur S Ramachandran, Director of the Centre for the Brain and Cognition, University of California, San Diego, tells us that vision in animals and humans evolved to defeat camouflage. Our brains evolved in highly camouflaged environments. We have a brain tuned to the unravelling and decoding of complex patterns and surfaces. For us to survive predation and find food the act of pattern recognition and deriving meaning needs to be pleasing. Our orientation towards evaluating surfaces and the significance of material patterns has a biological origin.[5] Materials then are significant in the role they play in contributing to the complexity and meaning we are constantly searching for. Outlines and suggestions need to grab our attention if we are to survive and reproduce.

Hyper Lounge Inflatable Ceiling Detail   Michael Trudgeon and David Poulton

Returning to the rug, the act of design or architectural intervention is akin to the drawing of a line in the sand. Territories are created by such gestures on either side of that line. Their significance may be perceptual, proprietorial, social or organisational, demarcating significant differences. How that line is understood, elaborated on, processed, expanded and celebrated becomes part of the momentum of the social context or event space that also creates the impetus for such actions and sustains them.

For Raymond Lowey and the skin doctors of early American industrial design the material boundary or surface was an expression of efficiency and optimism. It presented a slippery simplicity, obfuscating the complex internal uncertainties of the mechanical within.6 This opaqueness stands in strong contrast to the contemporary trend to expose and dramatise these processes through the use of transparent and translucent skins. While adding nothing to the users understanding of the machine this dramatisation can be engaging and diverting. Transparency is a connection of complexity and lucidity, creating dialectic between fact and allusion.

The notion of the surface as an expression of the material presence, a fixed skin, a stable and opaque signifier by which the viewer recognises and knows the entity or object has given us the model of the classical body. Communication technology, medical imaging techniques, remote sensing and computer enhanced visualisations give us the extended body, the body as data set, the enhanced body, the virtual body, the immersed body and the lost body. This transformation and augmentation in identifying and specifying objects, buildings and spaces has fuelled the pursuit of process driven indeterminate boundaries and surfaces.

For the architect Cedric Price the idea of a building is pursued and understood as a system of environmental control rather than as an enclosure or legible envelope. The building or boundary is seen as performative, designed to catalyse and accommodate change. The meaning or content of the space is expressed through transaction, the process of information exchange.[7]

Here the building is significant as a generator or filter. The surfaces are not passive markers but dynamic fields that mediate or stimulate the flow of information, inviting experience. This fusion of material and information we might call materiamatics.

Jeremy Rifkin,[8] in *The Age of Access*, identifies the rise of the experience economy and a world informed by contingency and indeterminacy, a world not of truths but scenarios and options. Within this protean reality the world is full of responsive, shape shifting identities and personae, an entirely performative perspective.

Computer rendering packages have allowed designers and architects to celebrate this desire for an indeterminate, diaphanous shimmering skin, offering, like the dance of the seven veils, a glimpse of something unimaginably exquisite, something forever shifting and changing; an enfolding plasma membrane.

The idea of the blurred and porous boundary, somehow responsive, eliciting intrigue while at the same time being inexpensive and easy to detail has been preoccupying our studio. For a recent commission we developed nomadic and reconfigurable semi-private media viewing pods or digital cinema capsules for use in a public museum space dedicated to exhibitions of the moving image in Melbourne. These screen lounge pods have been designed for use by small groups of people to view video on demand, play computer games, surf the net and produce their own content for viewing by others within the museum.

The pods were designed to respond spatially to the demands generated by the burgeoning presence of digital space. The project seeks to explore or identify an in-between space where people can interact with digital spaces and narratives. It has seemed to us that the digital environment and the physical one are evolving in a parallel yet strangely disconnected way. The interface in digital parlance is understood as the Graphical User Interface, not the space the user must inhabit to connect to the digital domain. We have sought to address the social, psychological, physiological and haptic dimensions of this connection. We began with the typology of the domestic lounge room and have enfolded elements of this into our design, some translated into digital systems and sometimes used as envelopes to accommodate digital systems and equipment. We have finished by contemplating the domestic lounge room as a digital production facility, an information receiving and information generating space. In hyper lounges you not only can watch and interact with digital media you are also expected to produce digital material, be it art, narrative or reflection. This material can be displayed within the pod, stored or broadcast to a wider network.

In designing these spaces we were keen to emphasise the idea of the flow of data and energy through the building spaces, to create spaces that were not readily determined immediately, with the intention of creating curiosity, with surfaces that wrapped around the lounge spaces but did not isolate them. Drawing from the vocabulary of video and film production we wanted to design an exterior skin that reflected this character, alluding to scanning, sampling and the jump cut, to create a discontinuous and fragmented porous surface that suggested the voyeuristic and participatory nature of television. We also saw this discontinuous nature as being more generally reminiscent of the experience of the city.

This project has, for us, been a focus for the idea of linking information to material space as well as virtual space. In seeking to link these we have created story telling and story making spaces. It is our attempt to extend the possibilities of the rug, to fold them into the magic carpet and the taxi, and to see where it takes us.

Hyper Lounge Pods, Australian Centre for the Moving Image   Michael Trudgeon and David Poulton

1   Alan C Kay, 'The early history of smalltalk', in *History of Programming Languages II*, T Bergin, R Gibson (eds), New York: ACM Press, 1996.

2   Ezio Manzini, *The Material of Invention*, Cambridge: The MIT Press, 1986.

3   Raymond Williams, Keywords. *A Vocabulary of Culture and Society*, New York: Oxford University Press, 1976.

4   Avrum Stroll, *Surfaces*, Minneapolis: University of Minnesota Press, 1998.

5   Vilayanur S Ramachandran, 'The emerging mind', Lecture 4, 'The artful brain', The Reith Lectures, 21 June 2003, BBC Radio 4.

6   Raymond Lowey, *Industrial Design*, New York: The Overlook Press, 1979.

7   Mary Lou Lobsinger, 'Cedric Price: An architecture of the performance', *Daidalos* 74, 2000, 22-29.

8   Jeremy Rifkin, *The Age of Access*, London: Penguin, 2000.

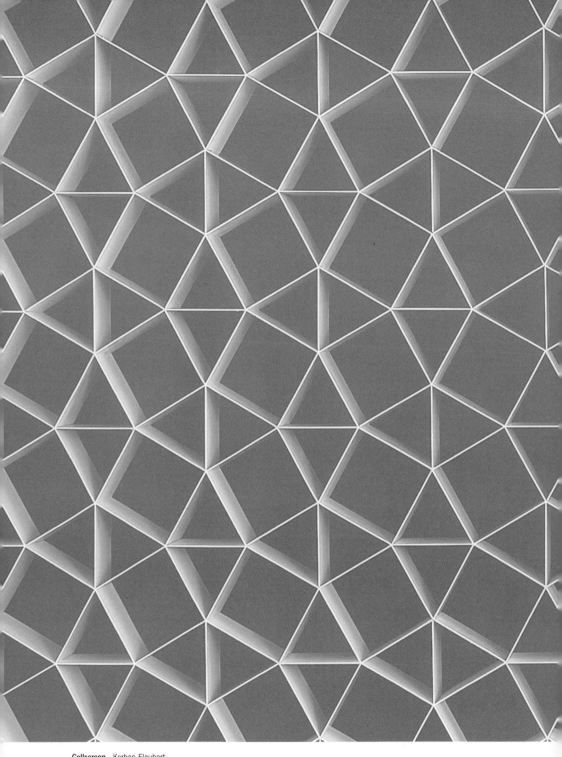

Cellscreen Korban Flaubert

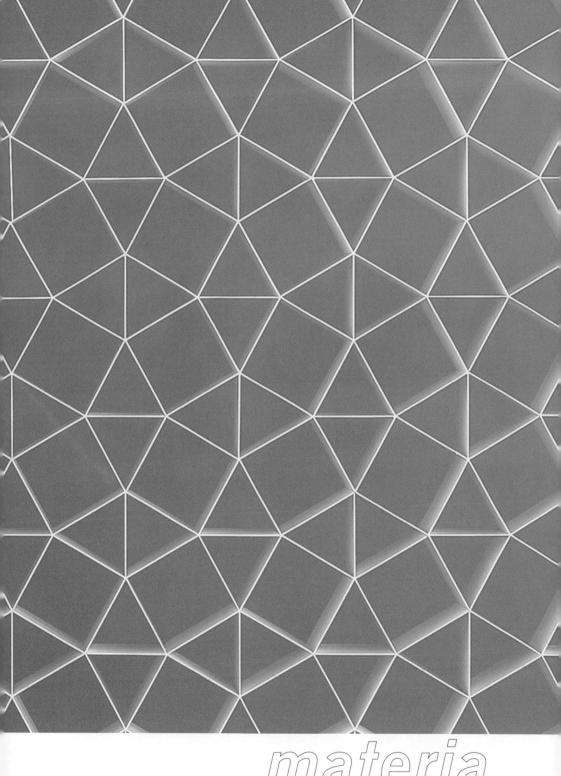

materia

Workshop as Laboratory

Janos Korban

Korban Flaubert's approach to design generally involves more doing than talking, so it's a bit of a challenge to express it in words. It's not that were a bunch of illiterates but we're a small group who work together well and know each other well and often we just communicate in one-word or two-word sentences.

We're interested in the effect objects have on the viewer. How people face-off with objects and make sense of them. We're interested in primitive and instinctive responses and the idea that there are fundamental effects that objects have on all of us on some basic instinctive level. We want to make objects that are understandable on this level and that are understandable to anybody.

What we usually are aiming for is a self-evident result, an undesigned quality. We set up our workshop in such a way that our methodology would support this general tendency – we tend to invent themes and then set up experiments along these themes. And then they run, and run wherever they want to; sometimes something happens and sometimes it doesn't. Sometimes a product emerges and sometimes something more abstract.

The themes are often suggested by phenomena in nature, the outside world, life, the world around us. We don't set out to duplicate nature but it's pretty easy to be caught in the thrall of the natural world. Themes are often also suggested by material and action effects – by just playing with material. The workshop was set up first and foremost to be a place to have fun, so we play, we structure the play and then we play some more.

We can loosely describe our approach to design in terms of material and anti-material. On the one hand the effect of the material is of critical importance to the formal outcome while conversely there are projects where we rely on non-material, non-tectonic expression for their effects.

One of our main concerns is the idea that there is energy contained in the physical character of the materials. That is, the reality or the substance of the material, physical and perceptual qualities specific to materials and their configurations and scale. We thought it would be interesting to have these qualities dominate typological concerns. Can materials speak for themselves, by themselves, with no design?

Metals are our main material. We do a lot of work in stainless steel where the material has its own power and it's the material that dominates. Material properties are conventionally expressed in engineer's tables, elongation values, offsets, tensile strengths and hardness. This is something of an abstract and removed thing to be concerned with and having a workshop allows us to work directly with materials. Hopefully, after a while you can develop some kind of synthesised understanding of the dry, intellectual, physical knowledge and the actual hands on. We're always amazed that the more you know, the more there is to know.

The wrench project evolved from our first experiment along the theme 'material + action'. We wanted to see what happens when you take away the controls in normal tube bending processes. Everyone assumes they want smooth curves from a bending process but what if I don't want nice smooth curves? We set up hundreds of experiments just twisting, mangling and crushing things with no particular idea of outcome, just to see what kind of interesting effects would emerge. From these experiments the wrenchlamp product evolved.

We like this 'one material and one action' approach; the outcome is a direct result of that. It's very dry and non-mysterious and what you see is what it is. Our Membrane chaise-longue also demonstrates this in a much gentler way.

Another theme of ours is called Volume/Surface/Edge. It generally involves developing volumetric forms from flat sheet materials, examining continuity and the impact of edges. Tetra sphere is a single continuous surface with two edges. Swaylamp is a continuous surface with one edge.

A few years ago we were asked to develop a piece for an exhibition at object gallery Customs House on the theme of light. This was well-timed because we had been banging away with hard materials for a while and we thought it might be nice to work with something as intangible as light.

We liked the idea of light being a substance itself and being treated as a physical thing and making an immaterial effect behave like a substance and this generated our glowblocks: a series of blocks that generates fields of colour which merge differently depending on the viewpoint.

With the Bongo stool we liked the idea of making a blob that you could sit on, a blob that would firstly be a transmitter of colour, and second a material. It is moulded in polyethylene from a highly polished tool so it comes out waxy and shiny and can be produced in lots of fun colours and this is pretty much what interior designers specify them as – little blobs of colour that punctuate spaces.

Bubbles Korban Flaubert

Tetra White Korban Flaubert

Swaylamp Korban Flaubert

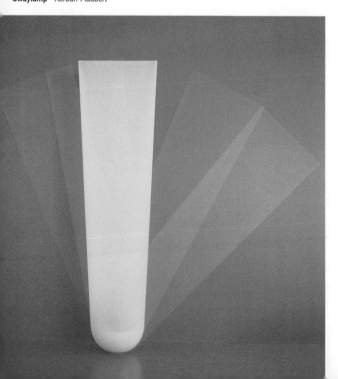

Bongo Stool Korban Flaubert

We're also interested in mesh and moire and the strange optical effects you get as your body approaches the pieces or which occur in shifting light conditions. The Siren piece began as an experiment in the manipulation of a single square of mesh. One of the models we explored ended up being a piece in the Sculpture by the Sea event, on a rock ledge above Tamarama beach in Sydney. At times it can look reptilian with its enormous variations in transparency; it's a quite a fascinating effect from a very simple mechanism.

With the cellscreen we were interested in making the material less material – it's quite a delicate structure and it has some of the visual properties of a textile or an Islamic screen structure but is executed in crisp, hard aluminium. Transparent from the orthogonal view, opaque from the angled view, so interesting effects as you walk by.

As the projects get larger we're interested in the effect that size has. Objects exist in a primary relationship to the body and its relationship to movement. Objects can motivate movement and engagement and they can activate your body. The site-specific piece we developed called 'arterial' is located on King Street in Sydney, directly opposite the Theatre Royal. We started out with a balustrade and we stretched the scope of the piece a little bit. It's now 16 metres long, made from 1.8. tonnes of stainless mesh. Here we were interested in repetition and sequence and shifting points of view and how these effects influence your changing relationship to this scale of object as you walk along it.

The site-specific pieces we develop are generally sub-projects within interior design projects or architectural jobs, mostly for corporate clients who have been intimately engaged with the process.

We like to make objects that are ambiguous and often have no function whatsoever and see where it leads us. We're interested in how this modifies the way in which people approach objects. You don't, you can't necessarily classify these objects within a known typology. It is quite interesting to see how people respond to that.

We spend a lot of time running experiments, quite basic experiments often, but they often generate interesting, complex results. Some turn into products, some don't but we have a lot of fun developing them. The projects oscillate between those that are very reduced and simple and those that, by contrast, rely on complexity and repetition, but in either case, the effect of material is usually critical to the outcome.

We like to know our materials really well and that's the benefit of having a workshop: beating them up first hand, and seeing what happens. But we'd never like to know them so well that they don't surprise us. We like to think that they always have surprises in store.

Cellscreen Korban Flaubert

Membrane   Korban Flaubert

Material is a Political Thing

Soumitri Varadarajan

Opening Story

On 25 July in a small town in Kerala, in the south of India, it rained. The rain was red in colour.

- The scientists speculate in the newspapers that a meteor may have exploded into a cloud of dust that hovered till the rain brought it down.
- Is a religious oracle somewhere using this as a sign that the Gods are angered?
- Are the environmentalists contesting the scientific interpretation, even as they await the chemical analysis of the rain, claiming it is the portent of things to come on this already polluted planet?

The scientist, religious Guru and the environmentalist each have a way of constructing knowledge. These three constructs I name the rationalist, the formalist and the environmentalist. And am promptly unhappy – because this does not help me construct the context in which the designer apprehends material. And so I restart my inquiry.

Red Metal Chair in a Paint Shop, New Delhi, 1989
Photo: Soumitri Varadarajan

Cycle Abandoned in a Park, Tokyo, 1991
Photo: Soumitri Varadarajan

Cycle Rickshaws in New Delhi, 1999
Photo: Prabhu Satyajit

Proposition: All lies

Different designers look at material in different ways. Some do not see any material in their styling exercises. Some re-dose society with its wastes, albeit peripherally, in the manner of unwanted material from hairdressers finding a resting place on the heads of the vain. Students all over strive to get an expertise in the nomenclature of materials believing it to be useful for their careers. On the fringes of design, the fashionable designers resurrect material and show it not as usable but as a curiosity, worthy of publication, documentation and exhibition. The digital mainstream in design is anonymous, silent and isolated from contact with material substances.

To set the tone I say that design in the past, as in the craft and architecture traditions may have been about shaping material. It is not that any longer, unless you are working with a craft community or with your own hands producing objects for sale on high street. Those who claim design is about material are lying. It is about profits, tapping latent desires, offering new lifestyles and about selling glossy expensive design publications. These publications are based on the assumption that the anonymous majority of designers in huge manufacturing enterprises are the silent audience for the theatrical performances of the designers who visualise curious rare collectibles. This particular form of design, mirrors media as a construct, and is also all about power of the sort enjoyed by the media personalities and their private relationships. This is power that does not look to exercise influence, at least not overtly, but can be experienced as an ability to be pervasive in media.

Proposition: On theory

I am taking up the task of depicting the space between the designer and material, if such a construct may be considered possible at all. This space can be given form and energised. The occurrences today of the many forms of this space in the profession of design need not be simplified for the sake of this explanation. Instead I speculate that a few instances can be discussed to energise the understanding of the designer's relationship with material. A construct here is a particular way of constructing design theory, with specific terminologies and concepts, and with specific sympathies and alignments. Material can be located in each construct, both as presences and absences.

Construct I – The bridge between matter and spirit is matter becoming spirit

Story 2

Years ago in design school I took up a project to design a conference chair for a building designed by an architect who in his past had worked with Corbusier in Chandigarh. As I did my research on the spirit of the building and what I would infuse the design with, I wrote up a statement of meanings that could be interpreted from the building. The two pages I wrote drew upon the terminologies that construct modernism. I was liberal with the use of words like truth, honesty and clarity in the use of material. I added to that Pevsner's condensation of the spirit into heroic, clinically precise and somehow machine-like. This sufficed then and continues to do so in situations like the design of furniture.

While still in design school I also encountered the official historical narrative of design. In this in the period before Bauhaus and Morris there was no distinct and separate use of the phrase Industrial Design, and history in a sense stopped here. However a loosely sketched narrative exists if you are shown that design is just a manifestation of craft, with a more industrial focus. What was made singly is now made en mass, but the spirit, the process and the role of the creator is still the same. I have often been uncomfortable with this, but have myself, in the past, propagated this way of looking at history to my students. My discomfort would become especially acute when encountering a collector of objects, textiles or carpets. This collector would typically be someone who was knowledgeable, thoroughly so, about the particular object. And every kind of object on this planet has a constituency of collectors. To listen to one of them speak knowledgeably about the balance, form and craftsmanship of a serving spoon and to see them definitively compare a set of spoons is a shattering experience.

In the collector's narrative the object would contain within itself the toil: a disciplined and trained hand skillfully executing the task while engaged in the pursuit of perfection. A picture that is at once simple and refined. We are invited here to dwell upon the instant at which the potter pulls his clay to make the form, the pot. It is here that purity is located. It is here that you are shown how in the act of creation thought and action, body and clay are not separated. It is here that matter becomes spirit. It is here also that joy is located, the joy of creation and the joy of materials. Since there is no room for corrective action or rethinking only redoing, again and again, the activity rewards a particular kind of temperament. One that is peaceful, relaxed, capable of being involved totally in what she is doing, assured and decisive. This portrayal is idyllic and perfect, and thus tragic too. For this is so hard to achieve for many of us because of the way present reality is constructed.

The way out we see in so many ceramic designers becoming potters, so many textile designers becoming fabric artists and weavers, and so many product designers starting their own workshops making limited editions. I went this way too, started my workshop and kept my hands on material, for a while. Till my desire to do stuff that I considered more relevant won out and I became a narrator. To become the observer who watched to see which of my students took up the tradition to connect with material.

Story 3

In 2001, a sculptor I was talking to mentioned that she was going to another city, to a block of marble she had kept there for the right time. Now she felt that time had come, the block was calling her. Though she had an idea of what she would be doing with it she knew that in all such circumstances things often change, the block might make her do something entirely different. In the above narrative the connection between the creator and the material is mystical and magical. This narrative exists today in design too, though in a somewhat peripheral fashion. It survives in art, vibrantly – though for most designers art is peripheral too. It survives in some design school curricula too, but its survival and transference is linked to either the persuasion of the teacher or to the absence of self-consciousness in the design student.

Story 4

What is more prevalent is a switch in the narrative. The designer is spoken of as someone slightly removed from the material, the mediator is the craftsperson or her proxy the machine. On a tour of a ceramic factory in Japan I saw a conveyor line of freshly formed cups still wet from the machine. A woman standing by the belt picked up each cup in turn and distorted it just so, with her bare hands. Later in the shop at the front of the factory I saw similar cups on display, each distinct and unique in its own way. This is acceptable too though in a somewhat impure way, as the surviving form of the chance processes that can characterise the craft object. And so it is that matter becomes spirit.

Construct II – All that is solid melts into air

Story 5

Years ago Chris Rust took me to visit a design company near Manchester. He had mentioned them as the contemporary face of design, and as an example of how to make a success of the commercial practice of Industrial Design. I saw a project there of a small hand held gadget for a South Korean company. From design to prototype the project was accomplished in twenty-one days, without meeting the client even once! The brief was electronically conveyed, the LC was opened in the bank and money transferred, concepts were done directly on the computer, the file was sent electronically to New Jersey for stereolithography and on day four the samples were being examined for refinement in the studio. On the twenty-first day the file was being read by a CNC machine in a tool room in Seoul. End of project.

And the material? ABS and naturally so. You ask not about the chemical identity but about the shared narrative of material, the historical construct, the tactile sensory experience. It's gone. In its place is the offset, of the CAD program. The cavity, the void, is a space that is to be injected and left to solidify. The texture is printed onto the surface of the cavity. The object will have a feel to it. A matte.

The preoccupation of the designer here is with the fitness to purpose. As functionalism – it is articulated as the principles of good design. This functionalism attains the centre by pushing material to the periphery. This is a process of substitution, rather than a decisive fracture, and design theory in most places begins to look like a menu of options. If there is to be a language of this design theory the terminologies have to be selected from a pool of words shared by management, engineering and design. Any talk of purity and material is embarrassing, and antagonises the relationships in what is seen as a cooperative venture to realise a new project. The object is a project.

Even the discourse on form breaks away and from being treated as inherent it becomes functional too. Psychology, semantics and semiotics support the explanatory framework. What was once a simple activity has become loaded with text, briefs, strategy, presentations and justifications. Transient publications that will be shredded or filed away in secrecy once the product is done. This situation needs a breed of designer who is a team player, one who surrenders possession of the project and hence the material to documentation. He is to be comfortable with the fact that he may never see the first product rolling out. And for him that is not what design is about. That is not it at all!

This is tragic too. So the peripheral existence of the unique object is resurrected. Supported by the knowledgeable elite, who are a new breed of collectors, the product for high-street grows vibrant. As expensive and exclusive for the discerning – only this comes as a reaction to the utilitarian. This is also a reaction to the displacement of material and the pervasive power of the functional to render worthless the sensory joy of the material. Crude and rough, often one off, these sorts of creations can be seen in the cast aluminum picture frames. Exposed unpainted metal!

And so it goes. The claims by the designers in the glossy design press can all be added up and in the historical narrative it can be constructed as a political discourse: the fight against anonymity imposed by the mega multinational work situation. The need to keep alive marginal discourses is supported by the pervasive desire for the consumption of the culture of the minorities. This mirrors movements elsewhere, like the spirited reaction to the loss of power perceived in the process of globalisation.

Thus it is all air (the void), the tangible melts into air.

The Milk Pot
Explorations in Ways of Handling Food
ShyamGadepalli, IIT Delhi 1997

Bins from Recycled Tyres
Thailand
Photo: Kim Scheufftan

Construct III – Material is a threat

Story 6

I am a garbage man (In 2001 I was collecting two tonnes of garbage a day!). As a designer and design teacher I am embroiled in the ongoing wrangle of freedom for each versus collective well being. The latter wins out in my recycling project and material for me is waste, the end, the problem and I have associates engaged in the sale of this waste material to agencies and factories which will either find secondary uses for this material or will reprocess and recycle the material. All this will happen before all material one day finds a final location as ash and air by incineration, or in transitory graveyards called landfills, or maybe in the future as projectiles to be sent into a still pollutable space beyond the earth's atmosphere. And we must not forget the traditional option exercised by the rich nations who for years have sent their wastes along with a monetary compensation to the poorer parts of this world.

When I first wrote this it was midnight in Kuala Lumpur in 2001. There were many of us from the Asia-Pacific region meeting to discuss how to get the world to consume less. One of the shared beliefs that brought the participants together is that materials are a threat and are essentially hazardous. Material is now a problem.

The shared narrative here looks with concern at the whole life cycle of a particular material: its extraction, processing, shaping into products, the use of the products and the final resting place of discarded products. Material is either seen to be the direct cause of an impact upon the environment or is seen to cause it in collusion with a set of other materials that come together as a product to use resources like water and electricity. Sanyo has announced their new machine will wash clothes without using detergents.

Elsewhere the focus of this view, liberally called green design, has been on the discarded product, the waste. This was seen as big loss of useful material. The consequences were that design would enable the dis-assembly and recycling of the product by the original product manufacturer. Referred to as closing the loop this did not always look at the whole life cycle of the product, which the generic framework of ecodesign then incorporated. In the project this mainly changed the stages before the brief was developed and not after. The process of problem identification became more disciplined and rigorous. Supported by software the environmental advantages built into a new concept could now be quantified. When this too was not enough the focus shifted to a product-less and material-less world.

The first stage in the path to a material-less world is when products are combined with services so that their overall quantities are reduced. The objective is being articulated as the reduction of the ecological footprint of an economic activity. Material being the necessary ingredient for most economic activity is classified and graded from the most harmful to the least harmful. Copper is bad and its use must be phased out because it is a scarce material. Plastics are bad because they are from non-renewable sources, finite and because cheap extremely susceptible to misuse, disposal and contain the potential to support a throwaway culture. This behaviour of plastic to litter and festoon the trees in the developing world drives the anti-plastic movements. Today many towns in India have a ban on the use of plastic carry bags.

The Annual Clock
Shyam Gadepalli, IIT Delhi 1998

Books - Professional Audio System
Soumitri Varadarajan, Denon, Japan 1991

The emerging discourse towards a less product heavy world is articulated as sustainable consumption, where we use fewer resources. With these paradigms seeping into the media and common usage many people the world over can make intelligent green choices in their buying habits. In a way the shopper looks at products in the supermarket as hazardous, the packaging will be waste instantaneously, the detergent inside will pollute the waters of the planet. In this the designer is offered the option to move away and practice design in a less harmful way. Designing products to be made from waste is seen as a tithe to be paid to society. Proposing an alternative aesthetic and promoting the classic style in an object that can be treated as a collectible are other ways to cut out the discomforts creeping into design theory.

'What can I do?' is the refrain that replaces the assurance of what I would like to do of construct I. And this is tragic too. Good design is given a bad name for the new good is the human one. Labeled social accountability the emerging theories of responsible citizenship permeate into the design discourse. Designers need not work visualising new forms of putting together the material, they need to be problem solvers where the better solutions are offered as dematerialised alternatives to what exists.

End Notes

On method

The three concerns I have articulated are depictions of the concerns of designers. Though it looks temporal and linear, it is not meant to be so. All the constructs exist simultaneously and are supported by society and academia. The staccato tone of the constructs was meant to open up the smooth narratives and definitive histories of design to alternative interpretations.

The palimpsest

And so it is that the design person's relationship with material is contested. Which of these perspectives should be privileged? All these perspectives exist simultaneously and are contextually grounded. And in the process the material becomes politicised.

Land(e)scape Casagrande & Rintala

Potemkin Marco Casagrande

Land(e)scapes

Marco Casagrande

I am an architect. I graduated from the University of Technology in 2001; however, I had set up the office in 1998 and lied to be an architect. I had a clear image of how an architect should look and how too work. I liked big ideas. However I found after six months that I was the first person to compromise my ideas and quickly became something that I had always hated, something like a prostitute, a very commercial architect just making money. It was my own fault because I was so weak, so all these big boys with money and politics would tell me what to do. So I stopped, like some kind of business hari-kari or suicide. I took all the money that I had earned and put it into my first project.

I wanted to construct something that nobody could come in between. It meant I would be my own client; I would be the architect, construct it, and finance it and so on. It then became problematic because I had to think what it was I had to say. Was there anything? So I made it quite simple. I went back to my childhood memories and things that somehow felt real.

Land(e)scape

Architectonic landscape installation realised in Savonlinna, Finland, 1999

This work was commenting on the desertion process of the Finnish countryside, which is happening everywhere in the world. If I go back to my childhood village in Lapland, it no longer exists, people have moved to the cities in the south. So I took three abandoned barn houses mounted on wooden shanks, raising them to the height of ten metres in order to give them a slow, majestic walk. Desolate, longing for their farmers, the barns cut their primeval union with the soil and were now swaying towards the cities of the south.

During this project I began to understand the value of process. I realised that one of the weaknesses I had previously was that I was just delivering plans and papers and losing the energy afterwards. So I became involved in the construction until the end, being able to react to the changes, to understand the structure's physical form and its layers, to be present. I have learnt a lot about this idea of presence from the circus, theatre and dance professions which are involved with being present, something that is lacking in architecture. I usually have other people from disciplines of art as mediators between the architecture or the physical form and people. Of course, I had to make construction drawings for the city for something that I had no idea how I was going to build, one of the basic things, to lie.

I had to make a timeline for this, to somehow deal with the energy, to make it more simple and part of the timeline. I wanted this humble architecture to have a chance to speak out loud. So I torched it. It was a strange feeling, of course; it is a very violent act to burn a house. So I put a newspaper advertisement saying that there would be free vodka and sausage. Six thousand people came. It was quite nice to see their reactions when the houses caught fire. It was really shamanistic or religious. Some people started to cry and maybe the weirdest was that some people were very confused.

This was very personal work and I didn't think much at all but it became some sought of icon for the desertion process. It was easy to be published in the media and when the pictures appeared in the newspaper it became the focus for a big discussion of the sociological changes in Finland.

Land(e)scape Casagrande & Rintala

60 Minute Man   Casagrande & Rintala

60 Minute Man

Architectonic installation for the Venice Biennale 2000

I was then asked to be exhibited in Venice Biennale in 2000. The theme of the biennale was 'Città: less aesthetics, more ethics'. The director Massimiliano Fuksias asked us to do an installation similar to the walking barn houses. I went there and was given this gallery space which was white and clinical and I didn't like it so I occupied the house next door, a much better ruin for the actual work in Venice. In Venice I decided to find a boat, an industrial boat to plant a forest inside, and sail with it from Finland to Venice. However it became quite clearly impossible, the vegetation would have died somewhere in the Bay of Biscay because of the very drastic climatic changes.

So we ended up in Venice with a Ford Transit with eight people inside it looking for a boat. It took some time. We found the boat in Chioggia, fifty kilometres south of Venice. Fifteen people working seven weeks took this abandoned old barge filled with mud and dirt to the shore, cleaned it up, made it waterproof again and made cuttings through the central axis to create a series of interior spaces. Everything we used was recycled.

We thought that doing this cultivated park in this piece of industrial waste wasn't enough so we decided that it should be built on compost. There was a big mystery as to what happens when you flush a toilet in Venice, there were many rumours. So we started to track down the digested sludge, to discover it all ends up in one place overseen by a very fine character. With him we calculated how much organic waste Venice produces annually. We then took it down to sixty minutes' worth, biologically cleaned this, composted it and put it into the boat as topsoil. It was under a layer of white gravel so when you first go to the boat all you see is these trees and shadows and it's nice. However when you go into the last room you see it's empty and in the corner there is a marble stone saying that this park has been planted on sixty minutes of human waste produced by the city of Venice. We sailed the ship to the Arsenale Harbour of Venice and it was opened as a public park.

Quetzalcoatlus Casagrande & Rintala

Quetzalcoatlus

Architectonic installation and exhibition at the 7th Havana Biennale 2000

I was invited to Cuba to do an installation and I came up with the idea of collecting 15,000 political, religious and philosophical books from all around the world, taking them to Cuba and using them as bricks for a construction. However I got a letter from the Cuban government saying that the work was unsound; you cannot take these kinds of books to Cuba.

But they were kind enough to give us the opportunity to do another architectonic installation without any kind of ideological meanings whatsoever. On the campus area of Facultad de Arqitectura Instituto Superior Politecnico Jose Antonio Echevarrira we built an installation, 'Quetzalcoatlus'. The name reflects back to the ancient times of Pteosaurs – the last flying dinosaurs. The living conditions turned out to be too hostile for these great creatures.

There were no construction materials to work with, so we took ten kilometres of fishing line from Finland and we knew that this iron bar was hanging around so we stretched it between two university buildings. The solid iron beam with the length of seven metres was tensioned between two concrete buildings with the fishing line. The distance between the buildings was approximately sixteen metres. The weight of the beam was 315 kilograms and it was positioned slightly above the ground level. The beam has its own flight pattern due the thermal changes which tightened or loosened the fishing lines according to the time of day and weather conditions. When the sun came out the iron bar got hot and the fishing line would begin to stretch and the bar would descend towards the ground. At night the whole structure cooled and rose back up again. The heavy flight of the beam was balanced on the edge of the impossible. It made a beautiful sound. One could sense the possibility of disaster. If you cut one of the lines away the whole system would collapse. This, in a way, represents Cuba.

Installation 1:2001

The book installation finally found its home as an architectural installation for the Biennale Internazionale dell'Arte Contemporanea di Firenze, Florence, Italy. The collection of religious, ideological and philosophical books from all over the world was constructed as a circular wall. The diameter of the circle was 6.37 metres (diameter of Earth 1: 2001000 according to Neil Heimler´s Principles of Science) and the height of the wall was 6.37:2 metres. The books were used as bricks. The names of the books, whether it be *The Bible* or *The Koran* or *Das Kapital* were facing the outside. There was one entrance so when you went in to the installation there was a white wall of paper, you could no longer tell which one was *The Koran* and which one was *The Bible*.

This, like all of the installations, was meant to be quite provocative, wanting to find a straight interface with normal people, to evoke feelings of something that they would remember and touch subconscious values. As we built the wall the Italian locals were looking at the books and asked whether they could have them; we said after the biennale you can have them but let the installation be for a while. But it took only thirty-six hours for the Florentine people to steal all the books. We had this security video camera watching the installation so we knew what happened, but the biennale organisers couldn't come to terms with it so they made this lie for the newspapers that anarchists and anti–globalists had attacked the installation. But the anarchists were more like grandfathers running away with five kilos of Lenin in Korean or Lithuanian, languages that they could never read. It was some kind of mass psychosis in the cradle of the renaissance.

Installation 1:2001   Casagrande & Rintala

Dallas-Kalevala

I was invited to do some work in Hokkaido and I had this image of the Japanese on the other side of the world being as far as I could get from Finland. So I flew into Japan and when I got to Hokkaido it was just like Finland. The climate was the same, the colour of the sky was just the same, the vegetation was just the same, the same kind of people and so on. I was really shocked so I looked at the map and found out that there was only one country between Finland and Hokkaido and that was Russia.

So I returned to Finland and drew a line to see whether it was possible to follow this line with a car. Of course it's a little bit problematic too just follow a line with a car. Our journey started in Helsinki, Finland, and ended in Obihiro Hokkaido, Japan. The trip was made by car, a Land Rover Defender. We followed roughly the borderline between taiga and tundra, cities and nomads. This is the climate area in which the northern civilizations exist.

As I traveled I was taking Polaroid pictures of grandmothers; every day I stopped the car and selected a good grandmother and took two Polaroid pictures, one for me and one for her. Every day I also traded a new axe in for an old axe. When I finally got to Hokkaido I exhibited the work in a horse stable with twenty-four stalls. The journey was twenty four days so I had twenty-four stops, twenty-four grandmothers, twenty-four axes, and also twenty-four times I recorded the local radio, if it existed, so people could make the same journey. To see how the grandmother and the axe are changing or remaining the same.

Dallas-Kalevala was a journey from today's existence back to origins of people living between Finland and Hokkaido. It was also a personal journey to feel genetic memory in places where people have always been moving between east and west.

Dallas-Kavella Exhibition   Casagrande & Rintala

Potemkin

Potemkin is a permanent park for post-industrial meditation in Kuramata village, Japan. It is a cultivated junk yard as a mixture of a temple and machine. It is articulated like a Zen garden except instead of rocks it is industrial waste. Recycled asphalt and broken glass make up the gravel. The park includes indoor and outdoor spaces constructed of iron; the deeper you go into the work the higher the walls become until in the end you are surrounded by this Kawasaki steel.

The park is situated, castle like, looking over the Kuramata rice fields and Kamagawa River. There is a small fireplace so you can fish in the nearby river and grill the fish at the park and go back home. It's a very small village and all the villagers can fit on the benches. It was really nice to work with them because they understood the work. They brought in a Shinto priest to bless the park. They have a dance they have been dancing for hundreds of years. All the villages get together and make this circular formation. It used to be in the Shinto temple but after this park was done they moved the dance here. Potemkin is a blessed and spirituous connection to one of the oldest Shinto shrines in Japan.

Potemkin   Marco Casagrande

Soft Stuff

Julieanna Preston

Wrestled from the auspices of upholsterers in the nineteenth century and serving to sustain a thriving industry of decorators, interior design appears to be assuming another dimension as a spatial and cross-disciplinary art. In the wake of such emergence lie numerous pockets of uncharted territory that promise to assert new forms, modes and knowledge of the discipline's practice. From my perspective, these positive developments reposition interior design relative to architecture, fine art, craft and performance.

The concerns for spatial and temporal qualities that hinge these bodies of knowledge together are bolstered by philosophical investigations on interiority and theoretical inquiry on the interfaces between social, political and geographical space and event. Interior design research and practice is taking an active role in probing these territories and by doing so, is charting its own body of knowledge.

Like all processes of maturation, lament or regret persist over what is lost, forgotten or transformed. Contemporary theory and criticism has noted the effects and faults of negating and denying historical inheritance in design. Equally so, aspirations run high to surpass the frontier of what is possible and imaginable in form and context – not simply for novelty's sake, but because modes of thought and accompanying technology suggest something other than what may be immediately familiar.

The work under discussion in this essay exemplifies a practice of critically examining the nominal aspects of interior design's past, its proclivity to decorate with colour and fabric and its commitment towards creating environmental comfort through design. New modes of interior design practice are pried open by delving sceptically into its own history as well as crossing into other disciplinary bodies of knowledge. As such, the work presented here is the product of design, in its active verb form, as the investment of knowing and knowledge.[1]

What follows is a discursive text on the work of sixteen third-year Interior Design students at Massey University, Wellington, New Zealand, 2003.[2] The initial impetus for this studio was based on my own cathartic shift from architecture proper to that of interior design. Such shift accommodated a long-term desire to give intense attention to issues of design often relegated to the margins of architecture: colour, comfort, light, ornament, social/political and cultural issues, and gender studies. It also served further inquiry on the relation between art and architecture, space and matter, function and event.

This particular studio is a place in the Massey program that affords a high degree of experimentation and open-ended speculation. This specific term approached installation work as a means of fusing full-scale and physical spatial construction with critical inquiry on the interdisciplinary nature of interior design. Installations offer a mode of working directly with phenomena, and literal and technical conditions of site and inhabitation. I demanded that our making work proceeded at full-scale so that the realities of comfort, craft and detail could not be glossed over or hidden by the abstraction inherent to representation. Installations are embodied spatial constructions.

The second motivation for this studio targets interior design's cultural and historical frame – that of interior decorators choosing fabric swatches and paint chips as appliqués to room surfaces and their furnishings. I was interested in addressing these contentious bits of interior design head on. My enthusiasm to embrace decoration and ornament with critical respect was not shared by my students who demanded spatial challenges more intellectually robust than stereotypes of the decorator's profession offered. And so, we bravely approached the topic with a goal to subtly subvert the practice, to set our sights on new definitions of disciplinary limits and to hopefully cull the sensory and tactile qualities of lived spatiality into our work. Ultimately, my own agenda is to uncover and/or to re-orient a means by which the softness of human comfort as wonder, bodily pleasure and spatial tactility can be intellectually aligned with ornament and decoration, particularly those associated with interior design. Together, my students and I engaged with issues of disciplinary boundaries – as Grosz writes: 'leaving the inside open for the outside to rush in and produce another inside'. And with that as our motto, the stuffed cushion became our studio's emblem.

Softness

Softness encompasses a range of spatial and material conditions:

- Soft to the touch, a tactile sensation, ranging from silky to spongy.
- Soft as an inherent material property, inferring something beneath the surface and quite possibly structurally related.
- Soft as a phenomenal event or temporal quality, a spatial ambience, such as light, sound, smell and memory. The descriptors 'delicate' or 'hazy' may be appropriate.
- Soft form, implying amorphous three-dimensional mass, volume or surface, perhaps non-Euclidean geometric form. Note this type's reliance on visual apprehension.
- Soft as a weakness, referring to lack of strength, fragile, indecisive, implying lack. Also aligned with marginal or peripheral.
- Soft as indeterminate or ambiguous, to do with boundaries and limits or more commonly understood as without reference, definition or point of origin.

Inferences to issues of gender, politics, cultural studies, technological innovation or philosophical debate within this list are obvious. As this list registers historic and stereotypical notions of what defines interior design, it also locates points of critical resistance or territories of speculative inquiry. While the list does not exhaust all of the potential of 'soft' definition, it is a by-product of literally working on the softness of four chairs.

These four chairs were both familiar and fraught with all the biases our intellectual pursuit sought to engage. They were proof of our stereotypical notions about what interior design was historically. As seemingly banal cultural artefacts they anticipated our concerns for material, construction, spatial and bodily inhabitation. They promised comfort. These chairs, donated by the Salvation Army, were well-worn, smelly, and held no pretensions about current fashion and all kinds of indications about past fashion.

Four practices unrelated to interior design were identified as well as methods of analysis associated with their performative activity. While most of these activities are focussed on the production of goods and services, we considered them as modes of material analysis, or in theoretical terms, deconstruction as a condition of reverse engineering. Specific tools, sequences and processes of taking apart, detecting or dissecting formed the basis for operating on each chair. The practice and its associated operations also became the strategy for investigating the cultural context of each chair and the keyhole to traversing theoretical inquiry.

Den chair

The first group of students examined a den chair as a physical and metaphoric landscape site in relation to a mining geologist's method of detection. A mining geologist surveys a territory looking for external clues of internal pockets of valuable fluids or minerals. A core sample is extracted at various strategic points in that territory to verify speculation. The sectional profile of such borings is analysed and scrutinised for traces of further evidence.

This project uses somewhat simplistic metaphoric analogy to survey the chair as a landscape terrain. The stained, soiled, collapsed and worn body of the chair was subjected to latitudes and longitudinal grid lines and literal bored for samples. The goal was to map the signs/site of wear and to discover what lay on the surface as well as below it without dismantling the chair and compromising future use. This exercise structured the re-presentation of the chair as a tourist map of conquest and comfort, a ploy that merged 'island culture' with colonial culture.

In many ways the group neglected to close the loop and speculate on the prospects of inhabiting the site, as land or chair. However, the arduous and meticulous way in which they surveyed the chair/land exposed the potential for interior space and interior furnishings to be analyzed and designed as continuous complex three-dimensional surfaces inclusive of their inhabitation residues. It locates a link between interior inhabitation and topographic surfaces, a reference demarcated by Cache.[3] The surface of landforms inclusive of their inflections and thalwegs[4] are sites for inhabitation as well as moments of spontaneous event and chance. Philosophically, such convolutions are made analogous to the continuity of a sheet of paper or fabric tunic as a territory of infinite folds, the basic unit of existence. That we could envision our interior environments as enveloping surfaces and three-dimensional matter, and design them according to complex topological mapping strategies informed by notions of inhabitation as 'bodies being in' is a territory ripe for design speculation.

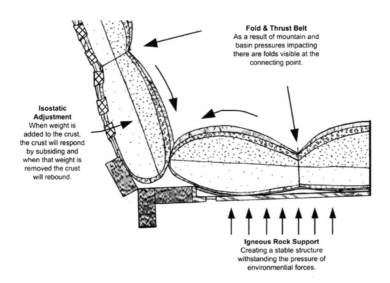

Fold & Thrust Belt
As a result of mountain and basin pressures impacting there are folds visible at the connecting point.

Isostatic Adjustment
When weight is added to the crust, the crust will respond by subsiding and when that weight is removed the crust will rebound.

Igneous Rock Support
Creating a stable structure withstanding the pressure of environmential forces.

Structural Formation of the Mountain and Basin

Den Chair as Landscape   Soft Stuff studio

Dining chair

As the patient and the victim of its own diseased history, this dining chair took on the practice of microbiology to scrutinise an internal body. A microbiologist takes very thin slices of a body organ. Documenting the whole organ in cross-sectional sequence, each slice is captured in a binding matrix and read in close detail for its internal organisation, performance and growth. The thinness of the slice yields transparency in its multiple meanings. A world of organic form, colour and texture are illuminated through magnification. Each sample is scrutinised for abnormalities.

Swab samples of the chair were literally brought to life and later identified thanks to the technicians at the university microbiology lab. Imagined realities and experienced conditions of hygiene and sterility in the samples and the lab revealed a proliferation of residues. Within the soft stuff of everyday materials there are abundant hosts of teaming organisms. As we nestle down into these absorbent surfaces we not only feed these macroscopic communities, we submit ourselves to their infestation. The cultural and historical propaganda on cleanliness which so profoundly impacted architectural and interior design suddenly gained value. Interior space and surfaces were no longer thought to be benign. Rather than appeal to the gross substances residing in the chair fibres, students used the visual beauty found in the illuminated slides to generate a series of material experiments. This act of 'seeing through' the matter maintained a clean environment and allowed the project to merge into the dirty of interior design: decoration.

Writing on this aspect of soft stuff in terms of weakness, Sola-Morales states:

> Decoration, then, or the decorative condition of contemporary art and architecture, not in the sense of vulgarity, of triviality, of the repetition of established stereotypes, but as a discreet folding back to a perhaps secondary function, a pulling back to a function that projects beyond the hypothetical grounds of things.[5]

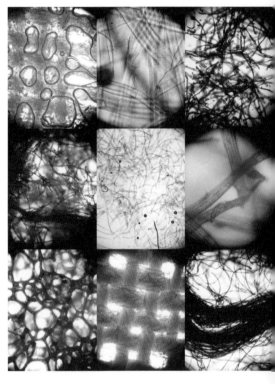

Dining Chair Microbiology   Soft Stuff studio

Analogous to the organ dissected for the sake of 'knowing' the whole body, weak architecture resists the classical condition of unity and wholeness as a system of cataloguing that curtails invention and distraction necessary for creativity. In the case of this group, the organ is sacrificed for the sake of realising another dimension. What is weak and soft has the potential to be generative. These students worked with common and banal materials by aberrant or 'germ infested' means, to subterfuge the banality of the material by virtue of revealing its potential to be ornamental and decorative primarily through tactile means. Concrete, plaster board, carpet and acoustic ceiling tile were manipulated out of their common institutional straight jackets and infected with unconventional processes and substances. As samples they were abnormal.

The diseased chair was quarantined in a sanitised room lined with plastic and stainless steel. The space was lined with images of its own germ cultures and the material samples. The images were enlarged and copied onto sheet film to repeat the magnification and transparency of the microscope and culture dish. The samples occupied horizontal surfaces like knick-knacks. As the images and samples filled the room, the room became smaller, cluttered and more inward focussing. Back lit from behind by a large window, the room was illuminated as a decorated shed. Such decoration exposed the potential for excess to be a spatial agent.

I started to wonder about the role of decoration in contemporary interiors. And convinced that it still thrives like a germ in even the most austere of published works, this group's work confirms Gombrich's assertion that decoration and ornament are intimately related to systems of order and mnemonic analogy.[6] I wanted to exercise various modes of 'tidying up' this shed, to find rhythms of pattern and colour, to sort this collection as a mode of inhabiting it and making it my own. And as the images and artefacts in this tiny, dense and almost claustrophobic room accumulated in the guise of design, they would become another instance of Semper's decorative enclosure. Would this incite a professional riot – that the practice of interior design is closer to the origin of architecture than more than one historian would like to admit?

Quarantined Chair Soft Stuff studio

Reclining chair

In *Wild Things: The Material Culture of Everyday Life*, Judy Attfield asserts that 'things' of the world hold object relations that interplay between the animate and inanimate worlds. She describes material culture of everyday life as the physical object in all its materiality as it encompasses the work of design, making, distributing, consuming, using, discarding, recycling and so on. 'But above all she focuses on how things have gone through all those stages as part of the mediation process between people and the physical world at different stages in their biographies.'[7] Design, according to Attfield, is a particular subset of the material cultural of things, one that distinguishes itself from most other things by investment of attitude.

This group took a very robust approach concerning the reclining chair as an artefact of modern popular culture. They established a link to the recliner as a lazy-boy (a gendered and branded La-z-boy) with that of butcher and pig. As they investigated the means by which a pig is carved into special cuts and packaged for retail consumption, they traced the relation between TV culture and TV dinners. After having prepared the studio for the slaughter, they cut the chair into the distinctive cuts and vacuum-packed the pieces into soft pouches. Every morsel of the chair was used with the exception of a few pieces of metal hardware which would not pass through the vacuum without puncturing the plastic wrap. In this case the students found an honourable means by which to both criticise the popular culture they claimed to abhor as well as to sacrifice the beast of a chair they could not dwell with aesthetically – even though, until it was carved up it was always occupied!

Cloth, foam, timber and steel, ground, minced and pulverised, one mass produced and consumed item was reproduced into another. A La-z-boy chair was processed into select cuts of processed goods. The chair's body was carved into soft seat cushions. Softness became a sign of material non-resistance and cultural complacency. Again, Attfield reminds us of the positive role that material culture can play beyond archaeological classification and historic data.

> The interdisciplinary encouraged by a material culture approach can prevent the conventional pocketed system of design classifications from forming intellectual backwaters as an effect of research that turns material culture to reductive static object analysis with no reference to the social life of things beyond the train spotter's collection or the museum archive. It also attends to the mismatch that occurs between the real thing in the real world against the aspirations of modern design theory about the democratisation of luxury goods through mass production.[8]

This group partially disdained the La-z-boy recliner because of its dominance in the market place and hence its status in popular culture and mostly, because of its unquestioned presence in most living rooms. Factory-made meant that it existed out into the design world like an aberrant monster in unlimited editions. So carving up by hand was their political resistance towards the commodification of design and body furnishing, a signal of their allegiance to Sorkin's commentary on the ethics of comfort.[9] The economy and production of making many sausages became fused with issues of sustainability, recycling and good old kiwi ingenuity.

Office desk chair

More so than the La-z-boy recliner, this office desk chair is a local product of mass-production. This group dealt with this via concepts of disassembly and assembly associated with kit-sets. They investigated the process of making the chair as an assembly line yet in reverse. As the chair was dismantled the pieces needed to be documented and catalogued. It was at this point that the exploded axonometric or isometric became critical to their practice. They likened their process of analysing the chair to that of an automotive mechanic who takes apart a vehicle piece by piece. Every part is essential in its relation to the parts around it. The process of taking apart is done in anticipation of putting back together. For these students, the space of inhabitation was the drawing and the logic of its parts not the bodily inhabitation of the chair itself. The drawing, the exploded view, however, does not relate sequence of operation as much as it indicates spatial orientation of parts to parts. The soft stuff was in the virtual apprehension of thing as a whole.

Students initially sought to replicate this chair, to repeat it in exactitude. Their desire to replicate soon gave way to impatience and in turn was overwhelmed by their eagerness to generate something new, something else, from the chair and method. They could not simply repeat without some intervention. They are not good factory workers, thank goodness.

Initial attempts to create accurate patterns using simple orthographic geometry led them to use CAD programs which quickly revealed not only the potential to go forth and multiply, the ease of consumer capitalism but revealed the spatial complexity inherent in virtual dimensions – that of layers, overlapping volumes, three-dimensional models as willing subjects to skews, distortions and creative mis-representation or intentional mistranscription at the push of a button. Insistent on working with actual materials and space, the pieces of the chair were fabricated out of copper wire frames and hung as floating elements relative

to a neutral white surface, a projective surface. In order to physically manifest the virtual attributes of multiplicity, a single lamp positioned at variable stations produced shadows of the hollow figures on the surface. Students recorded the compound extensions of the new chair onto the projection surface. They drew a copy using the very principles of drawing's origin. In that act of miscopying, they located a critical and creative production. Hillel Schwartz writes:

> Copying is ultimately imperfect, our errors eventually our heirs. The more widespread the act of copying the greater the likelihood of significant mistranscription. Genetic slip or evolution, scribal mistake or midrash, whatever we call it, miscopying raises hard questions about identity, security, and integrity. The same technical advances that render our skill at copying so impressive also intensify the dilemmas of forgery. We use copies to certify originals, originals to verify copies, then we stand bewildered.[10]

I regret that they did not follow through to build the new chair. But alas, perhaps the findings extend outside pre-conceived expectations? I wonder if they actually built a new chair in the projection of its shadow. Perhaps the new copy deviates outside of typology of chair and therefore is unrecognisable without abandoning formal attributes established by long histories of chair? It seems that the chair was truly exploded. I wonder if Grosz would consider such work a text, one that could be read as perhaps a modest little explosive bomb, one that 'scatters thoughts and images into different linkages or new alignments without necessarily destroying them'?[11]

Exploded View – Office Desk Chair   Soft Stuff studio

Acknowledging the risks and pitfalls of applying theory as opposed to using it, I have some inkling that this work was successful in teasing out fruitful lines of inquiry and analysis by virtue of shifting between the edge and centre of interior design. I am not so confident that our work in the end fully addressed comfort from a sensuous intellectual standpoint and nor do I have faith or fear that these students will invest their designs with many of these forms of soft stuff. After all we are dealing with a century of 'good design', 'honest materials' and purity of form. These are not reasons to have despair. I found comfort in how at ease my students worked across disciplines and invested research as data or information into creative works. They demonstrated dexterity at crafting an idea from the givens and letting it fold and twist upon itself so that it was unrecognisable to its former self but still constituted by the same logic. The products and operations of this work provide a convincing case that sensorial conditions have an aptitude to engage with the intellect in concert with bodily comfort. And most significantly, the work demonstrated their working understanding of what interior design could be without needing to declare boundaries or prop up a manifesto to protect itself.

> ...boundary work is ongoing, from the point of making claims to legitimizing practices and judging outcomes. It occurs in all interdisciplinary activities from borrowing tools and methods to forming new hybrid disciplines...boundary crossing has become part of the process of knowledge production, not a peripheral event. Interdisciplinary work is in the discipline as much as it is outside them.[12]

Butchered La-z-boy Soft Stuff studio

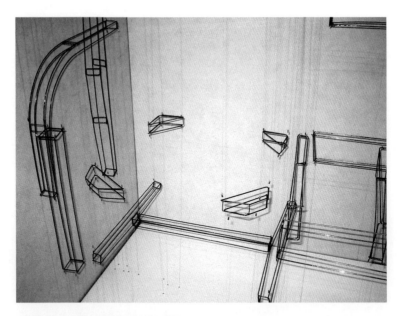

Exploded view – Office Desk Chair Soft Stuff studio

1 Peter Downton, *Design Research*, Melbourne: RMIT University Press, 2003, 2.

2 The students are: Joni Dawson, Stuart Foster, Charlotte Gardner, Gemma Gillett, Kathryn Gilmore, Nicola Habbitts, Sharlene King, Emma Lawrence, Mitch McTaggart, Emma Perry, Sarah Rowland, Richard Thurston, Natasha Wong, Ying Wang.

3 Bernard Cache, *Earth Moves: The Furnishing of Territories*, Cambridge, MA: MIT Press, 1997.

4 I am indebted to Emma Perry, a fourth-year student for this connection which she made in her final year Research and Development document 2004.

5 Ignasi de Solas-Morales, *Differences: Topographies of Contemporary Architecture*, Cambridge, MA: MIT Press, 1997, 69.

6 Ernest Hans Gombrich, *The Sense of Order in the Psychology of Decorative Arts*, Oxford: Phaidon, 1984.

7 Judy Attfield, *Wild Things: the Material Culture of Everyday Life*, Oxford: Berg, 2000, 3.

8 Attfield, 31.

9 Michael Sorkin, 'The Measure of Comfort', in *Comfort: Reclaiming Place in the Virtual World*, Larry Gilman, editor, Germany: Cleveland Centre for Contemporary Art, 2001, 1.

10 Hillel Schwartz, *The Culture of the Copy: Striking Likenesses, Unreasonable Facsimiles*, New York: Zone Books, 1996, 8.

11 Elizabeth Grosz, *Architecture from the Outside: Essays on Virtual and Real Space*, Cambridge, MA: MIT Press, 2001, 57.

12 Julie Thompson Klein, *Crossing Boundaries: Knowledge, Disciplinarities and Interdisciplinarities*, Charlottesville, VA: University Press of Virginia, 1960, 56.

Intimate Immensity   Andrea Mina

Why are Cuttlefish Tickled Pink?

Andrea Mina

For many years I have held a fascination for the architectural model, consequently I have enjoyed a rich relationship with these diminutive three-dimensional forms, be they in the guise of on-the-spot folded paper models used to illustrate an idea or the highly finished architectural presentation models I have made on commission. My interest in the architectural model has been informed and enriched through collaborative research undertaken in the design studio with interior design students. This has been an inquiry into developing of a better understanding of what an 'interior' model may be if the interior is freed from the limitations of conventional representations of architectural form. Concurrently I began a private practice of constructing small, scaleless architecture which was sited nowhere else other than on my worktable and for few reasons other than to satisfy a fervent urge to make something in the image of architecture (one of the consequences of working in an academic environment characterised by its propensity to engage with ideas and future projections rather than the tangible realities of the 'workforce'). At that time I did not realise the significance the small size of my domestic workspace would have in influencing the trajectory of my research.

This private activity has served as the genesis for my research which has subsequently been formalised and brought into the public realm through my enrolment into a PhD by project, the working title of which is 'Intimate Immensity: The miniature as spatial discourse'. The initial making was generated in an 'un-restrained' and critique-free environment through what is easiest described as an 'intuitive' way of working. My research is being conducted through an iterative process of making, thinking and articulating, giving me the opportunity to interrogate this initial collection of work and to subsequently speculate on the work's inherent potential to generate discourses.

These discourses have evolved and I imagine will continue to evolve through processes which are as organic in structure as are the discourses they attempt to generate. As the making has been predicated on work practices reliant on chance or serendipitous encounters and the discoveries made through actual acts of engagement, there are evolving stories to relate that are neither linear in evolution nor entirely predictable in their outcomes.

Photo: Andrea Mina

Models

My objects are not models of some other reality, they do not substitute for that which is not present and are not scaled representations of something else as they are made at actual size, full-scale, one is equal to one, neither larger nor smaller, and exactly the size they are. They do not conform to traditional understandings of the architectural model as they have no promise of a realised, 'scaled-up', future existence.

They may have connections to the Architectural Canon which has a rich history of the representation of ideas through scaled three-dimensional architectural-models. Architectural models have predominantly been used as enabling tools to give form to imagined futures as in design models and the 'city-apartment promotional centerpiece scale-models' whose main purpose is for marketing high-rise apartments sold 'off paper', the 'promise' of a predicted future. The model in the image of architecture has another manifestation as the literal re-presentation of existing realities. This is best exemplified by the high popularity of commercially produced architectural-miniature models[1]. Their popularity has spawned an industry to satisfy the demand for exactly scaled and finely detailed replica reproductions[2] of existing buildings whose already loaded spatial histories receive additional dimension through each and every new acquisition by collectors linked through the internet's global embrace.

Miniature

'Miniature' is both a misleading and useful word to describe or attempt to contextualise these objects as the word offers an intriguing ambiguity in interpretation ranging from re-presentation on a small scale, with the implication that 'an original' exists prior to the production of a representation of 'it' to 'the art or action, originally that of a medieval illuminator, of painting portraits on a small scale and with minute finish, usually on ivory or vellum; a portrait of this kind'.[3] The latter interpretation is the more useful application as the inference is that the 'miniature' is the original, it is neither a reproduction nor a stand-in for something else but it has a presence and integrity of its own. There is a rich and well documented history of the tradition of hand making work at a small scale. This may be exemplified through the illuminations in medieval manuscripts and the pursuit of the miniature through the miniature paintings of sixteenth-century Persian and Indian miniaturists, the tradition of Japanese netsuke and the extraordinary collection of Fabergé eggs produced in the studios of Carl Fabergé in Moscow between the late nineteenth and early twentieth centuries. Fabergé's objects are not only an extraordinary and extravagant display of the virtuosity of their handcrafted manufacture but they may also be seen as material manifestations of an ostentatious and isolated culture, they hover between what they are and what they may be imagined to be.

In *The Poetics of Space* Bachelard writes,' we should lose all sense of real values if we interpreted miniatures from the standpoint of the simple relativism of large and small. A bit of moss may well be a pine, but a pine will never be a bit of moss. The imagination does not function with the same conviction in both directions.'[4] Bachelard's understanding of the miniature provides insight into that uncanny ability of the miniature to act as a vehicle that can provoke and illicit imaginings that are vast in scale in comparison to the smallness of that which has evoked them; 'One must go beyond logic in order to experience what is large in what is small.'[5]

Hands

The initial group of work comprises seven pieces each of approximately the same size, the size determined by the immediate relationship between my hands, eyes and the materials at hand. The objects consequently bear a direct relationship in size to that of my hands; the size of one thumb, the breadth of my palm, a comfortable fit against the length of my thumb and three index fingers, the diameter formed from joining my thumb and forefinger and so on. I have subsequently been intrigued by the effects engendered through enigmatic scale and in particular those phenomena associated with or related to small handmade objects whose small size may be considered miniature, that special category of small, and it is to this end the objects I make are tending to become smaller and smaller in size.

When viewed in this context this work bears the direct handprint of its author, and in so doing reveals through its human imprint the unseen time and devoted attention invested in its making. That investment in time manifests its return by revealing the hand of its making and in so doing the artifact can only but-be imbued with an energy that resides as a consequence of this prolonged, intimate contact made between the skin of the maker's hand and the surfaces that give form to the artifact. One may well consider the time of making, the time of 'conversion into something'.[6] However inextricable this communion between time and praxis may be it is not reason enough to assure poiesis or in other terms creative production. James Corner states in an article in *Word and Image*, '...an important connotation of poiesis is that only through the sentient perception of tactile and creative activity – the actual work of making – can discovery and revelation occur, the longed for moment of disclosure.'[7] From this can be understood the depth of engagement demanded from the maker by both the time of encounter and the material in hand, for without either there is nothing.

Materials and tools

The accumulation of materials is an easy task as the volume of material demand is slight due to the very small scale at which my work is made. My materials of choice are those of which the origins are organic, ie at one stage in their existence they have contained life forces or were the channels through which some of the forces of life have been directed. Apart from my initial purchase of a length of 50x50mm balsa wood I have since not had to enact any monetary transactions in the accumulation of materials apart from the purchase of synthetic glues and adhesives. I have not intentionally sourced materials, preferring to allow whatever encounters to occur of their own making and in their own time. It is pertinent to reiterate the fact that a relatively small amount of material lasts a great distance when working at very small scale. To date I have worked with balsa wood, jarrah, pine, red gum, mountain ash, merbau, meranti, palm, plum, bamboo, kelp stalk, kelp pods, sea-anemone shell/spines, cuttlefish bone/shell (pink shell is highly prized) and cat and dog hair. Jarrah has proved to be the most resilient of timbers and the most rewarding in terms of being able to provide a fine diameter and long length. Bamboo shards as fine as human hair were a serendipitous discovery made by bending a length of bamboo back onto itself to the point of its sudden explosive rupture. Surprisingly one of my cat's hairs has provided the thinnest and straightest self-supporting material to date.

My implements are small hand-held manually operated tools apart from an electric dremmel and its assortment of sanding and drilling attachments. These tools include a Stanley knife and cutting blades, scalpel knives and blades, various sized and shaped tweezers, small pliers, small scissors, assorted dentists' tools, eg scraper, pricker, steel straight edge, solder-iron clamps and stands, sandpapers, masking tape, pva and 'super' glues and most importantly a number seven OptiVisor jeweller's optical headset. I am intrigued by the dialogue between glue and the organic parts it connects and brings together: order established through synthetic means.

Photos: Andrea Mina

Techniques

At all times there is an attempt to articulate space and its enclosing or defining forms as without one there is no other. Of most interest are the edges at which these two opposites meet, and in their meeting shape their coming into being. If we postulate form as defined by its extremities, ie the limits of its edges, it follows the shape of this edge signals visual clues necessary in understanding the nature of the form. I am interested in the shaping of these edges and the relationship between edges made with directed intention and those edges that emerge as a consequence of the method of their making; in my own making this is exemplified through the techniques of working materials to their points of imminent destruction, thereby producing edge conditions that emerge through forces beyond immediate control.

How fine can a splinter of timber be pared back until the bonding forces of its fibres are exhausted with the resulting disintegration of its material integrity? That ultimate moment of material rupture, the point of intractable destruction is a moment of pure resistance signaling completion through an abrupt, enforced ending to the action at hand. But it is only through these explosive moments that both hand and material limitations are exposed and apprehended.

It is also shaped from a theoretical premise of redeeming an 'architecture' at the point of destruction or disintegration through an intimate concern for its interiority. This is clearly manifest in the work through the literal working of materials to a point immediately prior to their destruction.

Doodles

I employ a method of working that is in many respects analogous to my passion for doodling with pen on paper. After many years of doodling I believe the best doodles are made through an initial response to something that happens to be already there; the results have a greater sense of immediacy and produce the most unexpected outcomes. It is and therefore it has potential and as such invites a response which may lead to an interaction that once again may or may not elicit another response and so on and so forth until eyes, hands and intellect are satisfied, satisfaction being one of the most enriching forms of resistance as without resistance there can be no end to an unfolding project. In most instances that resistance is time, however in my making resistance is literally the ultimate moment of material rupture, at the precise moment it breaks, that point of intractable destruction. This is a moment of pure resistance, an explicit moment, and one which signals completion through an abrupt enforced ending to the action at hand. It is through these explosive moments that both hands/eyes and material limitations are exposed and apprehended, with the knowledge gained through this knowing used to inform and refine future actions and encounters.

Serendipity

I would like to augment the above by addressing the idea of, and delight in serendipity, that 'making of happy and unexpected discoveries by accident'.[8] Serendipitous moments have been and continue to provide a strong influence both in the conceptualisation and making of this work. The serendipitous moment is possibly the most cherished of moments and possibly also the most illusive. 'It' appears without announcement, agenda-less yet charged with latency. The moment is heightened through the fact of its being and the fact of the impossibility of attempting the orchestration of its coming into being. These moments cannot occur unless there is an intense engagement with the material in hand. It is through heightened senses and clarity of vision that one is able to extract one's self from the task at hand to acknowledge the significance of that which has transpired. This requires acute perception and a heightened awareness of the order 'of things' to first apprehend subtle shifts and misfits in this 'order', but then, more importantly, to be able to identify and apply an 'appropriate fit'; so what is it asking to be?

Carving and enclosing

Two opposing methods are explored in the shaping and hence articulation of space: carving space and enclosing space. In carving space one works with a given solid by progressively removing material from the original to reveal an enclosing form containing space, the process of removal being able to take place from within and from without the original mass, ie the eventual form may emerge as a result of carving a form from a solid and then removing the interior mass to expose the object's void space. Or conversely a void may be carved from a solid and then the material removed from the outside in towards the void. In both cases the process of removal is continuous until the separation between interior and exterior space is abruptly defined through the failure of the material being worked with. A defining characteristic of the forms that eventually evolve from this process is the continuity of their surfaces; form is privileged over space. Enclosing space in contrast to the aforementioned requires the joining together of points in space through the assemblage of component parts; these parts are either handmade or are searched for in the workings on my workbench. Through the nature of its assemblage this is a process of accretion, the form slowly emerging in response to gravitational and compositional demands.

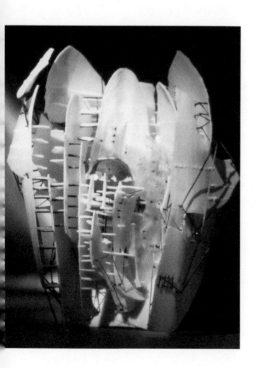

Photos: Andrea Mina

Dialogues

The work is not made with or according to specific narratives; if it is to have a life that life and its stories are momentary illusions which are entirely dependent on the perceptions, imaginations and mental projections of its observers. My work attempts to establish dialogue between material destruction and notions of material composition, construction and re-construction. This is one of many dialogues that explore tensions between interiority and exteriority, between durability and fragility, erosions and revelations and between the object and the frame. The work engages with these ideas of tension through the literal material and body tensions encountered in their making and through the instinctive bodily tensions which we experience during initial encounters and subsequent engagements with very small objects. These tensions are further engendered through hoped for dynamic fluctuations in apprehension that may occur as a result of juxtaposing opposing ideas within the same composition or frame. There is a fine balance between establishing a space of tension as distinct from establishing a space of oppositions because to engineer an equilibrium of material resonances within the same space requires the provision of a democratic space of engagement, a space able to accommodate the simultaneous material co-existence of not one but many voices in material form that is neither excessive nor lacking, thereby establishing dialogue in preference to hegemony.

Encounters

Whilst the scale at which I work elicits parallels between these miniature objects and the scale at which jewellery is made, unlike jewellery these objects deny any direct or immediate contact with the human body. Their seeming and actual fragility denies unsupervised handling; this is a fragility heightened by their encapsulation within the transparency of thin glass containers; they remain enticing and ellusive, being touched only by the brain and felt through the human eye. By virtue of their small scale encountering small objects places conscious demands on the negotiation of the space between the very small object and the relative gigantic scale of the human body. These encounters require the observer to slow time down, to exclude external distractions for the purpose of focusing attention on minutiae amidst the normal scale and complexity of everyday life. Bodies are subject to unusual stresses as they tense to maintain equilibrium whilst hunching and straining forward, slowly testing the limits of how close to approach at such a small scale, guided by vision and innate senses of proximity. Tensed eye muscles are accompanied by an instinctual forwards movement of the head as they are forced to limit their field of vision in their attempts to adjust focus at such unusually close proximity. A conscious effort must be made to control the random scanning of the eye so that the minutiae of material and composition can be apprehended and pieced together to form a cogent understanding of the whole. The effort, hence energy of this craning forward, is intensified through the unfamiliar demands placed on the muscles to control movements measured in fractions of a millimetre. The miniature demands a commitment from its observer which is in the form of an investment of time, probably the most precious 'commodity' of all.

Ralph Rugoff offers this description in his catalogue essay for the 1997 exhibition 'At the Threshold of the Visible' of the ability of 'tiny artworks' to 'force us to draw closer in order to scrutinize them, and this forward movement parallels a mental process: the more closely we examine minute details, the less we notice the gulf in size that separates us....This charges our experience of the object, imbuing it with an almost hallucinatory acuity.'[9]

Catalyst

One of architecture's most fundamental characteristics is its capacity to provide for and accept human occupation. If we accept we can and may be projected into extraordinary mental spaces albeit for infinitesimally small moments of time and in doing so virtually occupy two spaces in the same moment of time, then the work may be viewed in the context of a very particular type of architecture. This is architecture at full scale but at a very small and enigmatic size. Through its form and by the images it may evoke or project the work may act as catalyst and facilitator for momentary flights of fancy driven by personal narratives in the hope for those split-second moments of occupation.

To physically encounter the diminutive is in itself an experience of disjuncture. It is these immeasurable moments of virtual occupation that are the central concerns of this work and it is to this end that the individual pieces remain untitled, freed from prescriptive narrative, desiring to remain material instead of metaphysical.[10] Central to my research is the idea that we cherish within us an innate common architectural imagining capable of being triggered through associations and composition. Yet it is through these miniatures' overt architectural connotations and their strong assertion of interiority (and hence inhabitation) that there is aspiration in the making for the object to act as a catalyst for projections into this common architectural imagining and thus simultaneously, an occupation of those virtual spaces. These highly personal and infinitesimal spaces of imaginative flight are analogous to those daydreams described by Bachelard, 'Daydreams of this sort are invitations to verticality, pauses in the narrative during which the reader is invited to dream. They are very pure, since they have no use.'[11]

1 A recent Google search 'architectural miniatures' listed 62,600 websites, the majority of which are suppliers of architectural miniature related products and services.

2 Umberto Ecco, *Travels in Hyperreality*, Orlando: Harcourt Brace and Company, 1986.

3 *New Shorter Oxford English Dictionary*, 2003.

4 Gaston Bachelard, *The Poetics of Space*, Boston: Beacon Press, 1969, 163.

5 ibid, 150.

6 *New Shorter Oxford English Dictionary*, 2003.

7 James Corner, *Word and Image*, vol B, no 3, July/September 1992.

8 *New Shorter Oxford English Dictionary*, 2003.

9 *At the Threshold of the Visible, Miniscule and Small-Scale Art*, 1964-1996, New York: Independent Curators Incorporated, 14.

10 Conversation with Peter King, 28 April 2003, '(the work) pushes desire to the brink of meta-physical meaning.'

11 Gaston Bachelard, *The Poetics of Space*, Boston: Beacon Press, 1969, 162.

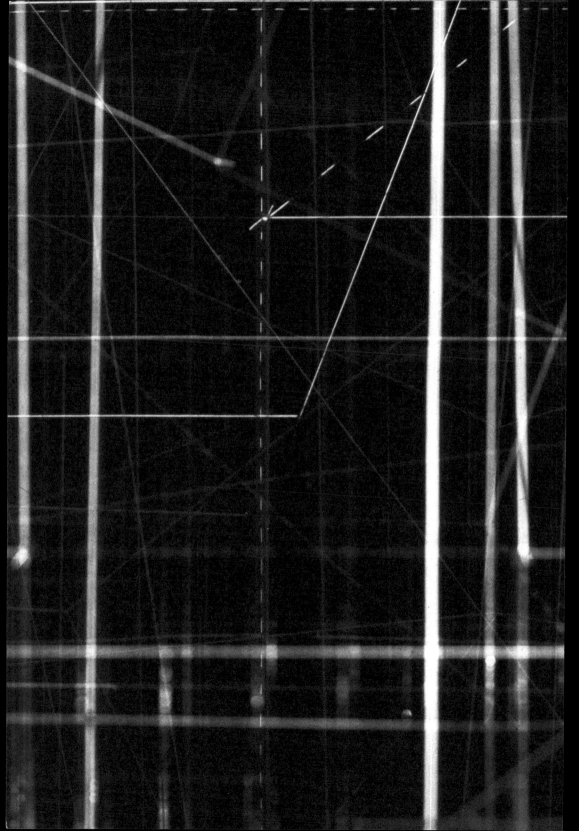

Designing for the Sensuous Intellect

Robyn Ho

The 'Sensuous Intellect' is described as existing in the gap between sensation and thought, visceral bodily reactions giving rise to perception.[1] To design for the sensuous intellect is to construct situations where such phenomena can occur. This emphasis on the response of the body suggests an embodiment of the viewer in relationship to the work being presented, an empowerment of the intuitive body over the rational brain of thought.

Yet designing for a sensuous intellect is to design to a process that inhabits the middle space between the immediacy of sensation and the variable time of thought. To embody the participant yet disembody them, as they are encouraged to inhabit the virtual formless space of thought. Appealing to the sensuous intellect is to affirm contradictions, not to assert one view, but many simultaneously, their synthesis creating the participants' perception, a middle ground that will exist in the 'gap between sensation and thought'. This mirrors the processes of bodily experience, as humans sense their surroundings by '...no individual mode of sense alone, but all senses simultaneously...it is about intensity.'[2]

To design for the sensuous intellect is to embody

With any encounter, one must gauge the material with the most primal tool of perception – the senses – as our bodies and '...skin are the start of our relationship with the world'.[3] It is the basis of the human cognitive processes to develop methods of understanding external information that stimulate the brain and give rise to thought. However, this process occurs quite subconsciously and without much consideration of the visceral interaction between the senses and its stimuli. One does not ponder much on the individual characteristics of a smell, taste, sight, touch or sound, but the brain immediately skips to the cognitive processes which identify the source of the stimulus. Humans focus on the cognitive result rather than the experience.

To create works in order to primarily speak to the senses is to make the participants' awareness of that initial procedure. If the viewer cannot recognise the usual signs that trigger patterns of thinking, then the viewer is forced by situation to utilise their senses. This empowers the body as it becomes the primary tool of perception, as if the work has coerced the viewer into 'listening' to their senses. An embodiment of the viewer occurs as they become aware of their body and the viewer no longer exists as an amorphous objective Eye but as an active Viewer that exists in time and space and that interacts with the work. That embodiment also occurs for the creator as '...in creative work, the scientist and the artist are directly engaged with their body and existential experience...' [4] However, interaction suggests an exchange, two parties giving and receiving. 'The encounter of any work of art implies a bodily reaction. A work of art functions as another person with whom we converse.' [5] Therefore, in creating sensual art works or architecture, the designer embodies the work, providing the construction an active role, a 'life-force', a body.

To design for the sensuous intellect is to disembody

Any creation ultimately intends to speak of some concept or idea. The space for thought is often externalised from the corporeal body, with no boundaries of matter or time, as '...you exteriorise perception from the body so that things become objects in space'.[6] This is not to say that concepts are not '...schematic structures that emerge from our bodily experience',[7] but thought transcends the boundaries of the body and exists almost separately and outwardly. As the viewer processes the sensual information, the act of imagination transports that initial information into those 'schematic structures' that do not tangibly exist within the body. These schematic structures contain a series of recognition patterns which the information is compared to and some level of cognition is reached. Thought acknowledges the need for the body but in its cognition development, does not require the use of the physical body. Emphasis on '...the intellectual and conceptual dimensions of architecture further contributes to a disappearance of the physical, sensual and embodied essence of architecture'.[8] Abstraction and conceptualism divorces the viewer from the boundaries of their actual bodies and the work and forces them to inhabit a boundless space of thought. Thought is an intangible construct, a visualisation that ensues from the tangible sensual stimulus of the work, the experience. Therefore, the viewer is embodied by the use of their bodies in the experience of the work, but then is disembodied as they are forced to think in a space outside or without their physical bodies.[9]

To design for the sensuous intellect is to deal with the now

Sensual responses are of the now. Human senses are binary in the fact that they are either on or off, seeing or not seeing, and so forth. To design for the sensuous intellect is to construct moments of intense presentness, the moment of meeting between two interfaces, one of the viewer's body, and one of the works.[10] 'The surface is where most of the action is…The surface is what touches the animal, not the interior.'[11] That interaction with that surface only lasts for the duration of that touch, or sight, and does not extend past that, as a sensual experience can only be spoken in terms of what it is or was at that particular time as the occurrence of the sensual situation can only occur when those particular variables happen together. Designing a work that appeals to the senses is to construct a field whereby these momentary collisions can occur. 'On principle, phenomenology liquidates the past and confronts what is new'.[12] However, that collision of surfaces becomes a cataclysm for thought, which has associations with the past and of memory.

To design for the sensuous intellect is to deal with the past

The sensual interaction of the viewer and work gives rise to thought as the current sensual experience is then compared to 'schematic structures'. These 'schematic structures' can also be called memory or knowledge. When confronted with recognisable situations, one is familiar with the patterns of signs, yet when something new is encountered, new patterns are created and existing patterns are then altered.[13] It is this shift of existing ideas that is the intent of any creation, the birth of new ideas. Concepts do not exist without some precedent that they have developed from, as thought does not exist as discrete moments unaffected by previous ideas but arises from the exploration of those foundation theories. 'All experience implies the acts of recollecting, remembering and comparing',[14] as '…memory is important to perception as it brings past into the present – the folding of various durations'[15] in the comparison of the current stimuli.

The senses, especially smell, evoke memory and nostalgia more effectively than any other method of communication. As Pallasmaa recalls, 'I cannot remember the appearance of the door to my grandfather's farm-house from my early childhood, but I do remember the resistance of its weight, the patina of its wood surface scarred by a half century of use, and I recall especially the scent of home that hit my face as an invisible wall behind the door'.[16] This nostalgia and history is also evident in the use of materiality by architects, for example, Leonie Matthews' use of fibreboard sheeting in her architecture as she associates that material with 1950s beach houses of the Gold Coast which are part of her childhood memories.[17] To utilise immediate sensation and feeling in design is to enable recollection and activate the past.

To design for the sensuous intellect is to design with disassembly

In exploring any proposition, one must break it down into its parts in order to understand the ways its components relate together to create the desired result. Consequently, to utilise sensual stimuli as a communication tool for any creative work is to analyse and test the individual senses in order to apply them effectively and to understand their capabilities. As can be seen in this manifesto and in the Sensoria conference itself (with its breakdown of experience into phenomena, media and materia), the analysis of methods of designing for the sensuous intellect involves the separate investigation of component parts.

To design for the sensuous intellect is to design simultaneity

However, one must remember that '…discrete items only exist if plucked from a continuum…'[18] and that an accurate depiction of sensual experience is not distinct. Sensual perception is not of focused vision but a culmination of a numerous points of stimuli that occur concurrently which immerses the participant. It is from the analysis of how this information can relate that the synthesis of all stimuli can be achieved, giving rise to thought and a singular concept, and possibly the middle point between sensation and thought.

Designing for the sensual intellect is to allow for corporeal bodily reactions and for cognitive intangible constructs to arise. The two words that make up the term are on some level contradicting each other, and that is an indication of how to approach design for the sensuous intellect – to affirm contradictions in order to find a middle ground.

1 Paraphrase of Trish Pringle, 'Phenomena Symposia introduction', in *Sensoria: Festival of Design Education – Phenomena Symposia*, RMIT Storey Hall, Melbourne, 27 July 2004.

2 Pia Ednie Brown, 'Emergent Forms of Experience', in ibid.

3 Michael Trudgeon, 'Smart Futures', in *Sensoria: Festival of Design Education – Materia Symposia*, RMIT Storey Hall, Melbourne, 29 July 2004.

4 Juhani Pallasmaa, 'Hapticity and time: Notes on fragile architecture', in *AR*, 1999, 4 (originally presented at 1999 RIBA Discourse Lecture).

5 Juhani Pallasmaa, 'An Architecture of the Seven Senses', in *Architecture and Urbanism*, July 1994, 25.

6 Ted Krueger, 'Human environment interaction', in *Sensoria: Festival of Design Education – Phenomena Symposia*, RMIT Storey Hall, Melbourne, 27 July 2004.

7 Johnson quoted in ibid.

8 Juhani Pallasmaa, op cit, 21.

9 Though according to Robyn Hampton, 'Thinking is not all in the head', but is linked to the movement of the body, which in turns embodies or gives a body to the thought process. This does not disrupt the thesis of this text, but just reaffirms the simultaneous contradictions of designing for the sensuous intellect. Robyn Hampton, in 'Brain Gym', in *Sensoria: Festival of Design Education – Phenomena Symposia*, RMIT Storey Hall, Melbourne, 27 July 2004.

10 Paraphrase of Pia Ednie Brown, op cit.

11 James J Gibson, *The Ecological Approach to Visual Perception*, Boston: Houghton Mifflin Company, 1979, 23.

12 Gaston Bachelard, *The Poetics of Space: The Classic Look at How We Experience Intimate Places*, Boston: Beacon Press, 1994 (orig. published 1958), xxxii.

13 Paraphrase of Pia Ednie Brown, op cit.

14 Juhani Pallasmaa, op cit, 25.

15 David Thomas, 'Duration of light', in *Sensoria: Festival of Design Education – Phenomena Symposia*, RMIT Storey Hall, Melbourne, 27 July 2004.

16 Juhani Pallasmaa, op cit, 23.

17 Leonie Matthews, 'A theoretical approach to material', in *Sensoria: Festival of Design Education – Materia Symposia*, RMIT Storey Hall, Melbourne, 29 July 2004.

18 David Thomas in 'Duration of light', op cit.

Zaishu Laser-cut Panels   Matthew Butler